Cinqué of the *Amistad*
and the Slave Trade in World History

Titles *in World History*

Cinqué of the *Amistad* and the Slave Trade in World History
0-7660-1460-6

Commodore Perry Opens Japan to Trade in World History
0-7660-1462-2

Cortés and the Conquest of the Aztec Empire in World History
0-7660-1395-2

Lenin and the Russian Revolution in World History
0-7660-1464-9

Leonardo da Vinci and the Renaissance in World History
0-7660-1401-0

Mahatma Gandhi and India's Independence in World History
0-7660-1398-7

Nelson Mandela and Apartheid in World History
0-7660-1463-0

Philip II and Alexander the Great Unify Greece in World History
0-7660-1399-5

Pizarro and the Conquest of the Incan Empire in World History
0-7660-1396-0

Robespierre and the French Revolution in World History
0-7660-1397-9

Stanley and Livingstone and the Exploration of Africa in World History
0-7660-1400-2

In World History

Cinqué of the *Amistad* and the Slave Trade in World History

Richard Worth

Enslow Publishers, Inc.
40 Industrial Road
Box 398
Berkeley Heights, NJ 07922
USA

PO Box 38
Aldershot
Hants GU12 6BP
UK

http://www.enslow.com

Library of Congress Cataloging-in-Publication Data

Worth, Richard.
Cinque of the Amistad and the slave trade in world history /
Richard Worth.
p. cm. — (In world history)
Includes bibliographical references and index.
ISBN 0-7660-1460-6
1. Cinque—Juvenile literature. 2. Amistad (Schooner)—Juvenile literature. 3. Slave insurrections—United States—Juvenile literature. 4. Antislavery movements—United States—History—Juvenile literature. 5. Slave trade—America—History—Juvenile literature. 6. Slave trade—History—Juvenile literature. [1. Cinque. 2. Amistad (Schooner) 3. Slave trade. 4. Slave insurrections. 5. Antislavery movements.] I. Title. II. Series.
E447.W67 2001
326'.0973—dc21 00-009719

Printed in the United States of America

10 9 8 7 6 5 4 3 2 1

To Our Readers:
All Internet Addresses in this book were active and appropriate at the time we went to press. Any comments or suggestions can be sent by e-mail to Comments@enslow.com or to the address on the back cover.

Illustration Credits: Beinecke Rare Book and Manuscript Library, Yale University, pp. 82, 87; Enslow Publishers, Inc., pp. 6, 20; Library of Congress, pp. 9, 12, 18, 23, 24, 27, 30, 48, 50, 56, 58, 59, 64, 71, 77, 80, 83; National Archives, pp. 63, 94; Reproduced from the *Dictionary of American Portraits*, Published by Dover Publications, Inc., in 1967, pp. 89, 93, 101.

Cover Illustration: Library of Congress (Portrait of Cinqué); © Digital Vision Ltd. (Background).

Contents

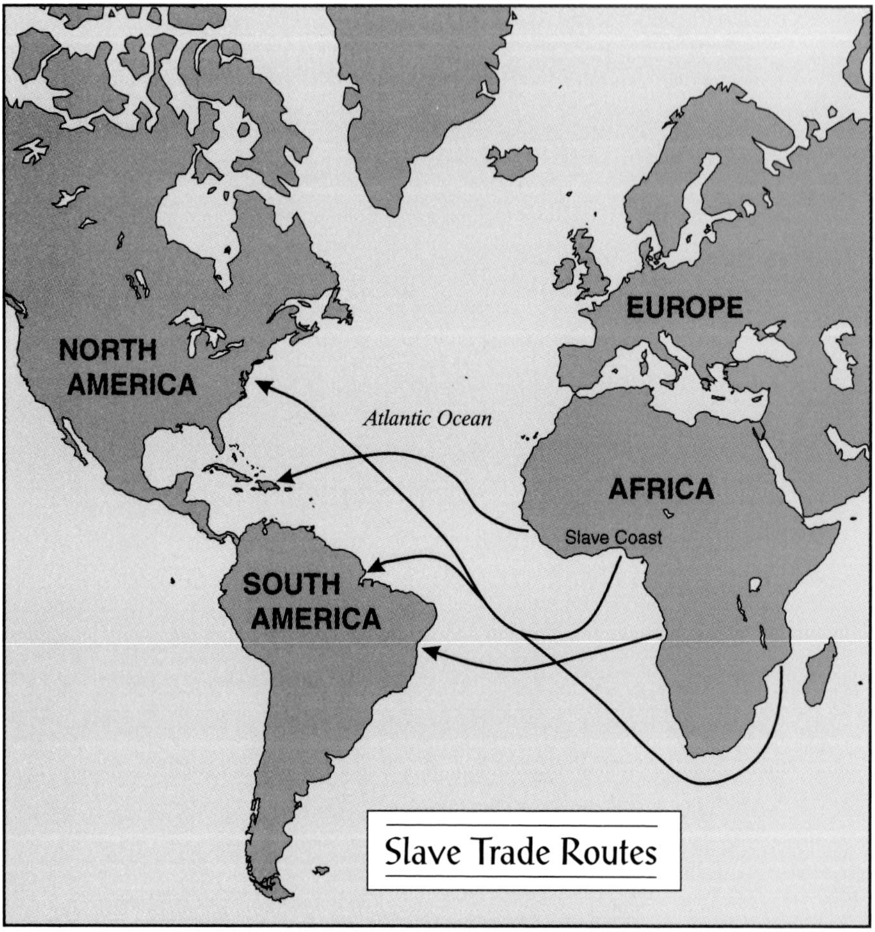

The slave trade operated in a triangular fashion. Slaves were brought from Africa (as seen above) to work in the fields of America, then crops grown in America were shipped to cities in Europe, then trade goods from Europe were exchanged for more slaves in Africa.

Chapter 1

Rebellion!

For twenty-five-year-old Joseph Cinqué, it had been a long and frightening journey. Cinqué was a rice farmer in Sierra Leone, Africa. Early in 1839, he had been seized along a lonely road near his village in Mende country by four men he did not know. Led away in chains, Cinqué had eventually arrived on the west coast of Africa. There, he was roughly herded into a barracoon—slave barracks—with other Africans who had also been stolen away from their families. There were men, women, and children—frightened at having been taken away from their homes. Although they did not yet know it, all of them were bound for a life of slavery.

Each of these people had become the prisoner of Don Pedro Blanco, the wealthiest slave trader in the district. Representing a powerful slave trading organization based in Havana, Cuba, Don Pedro lived in great luxury at the mouth of the Gallinas River on the African coast. As historian Daniel Mannix explained:

> Don Pedro kept a stock of more than a thousand slaves in ten or a dozen barracoons on a series of marshy islands. On another island near the mouth of the Gallinas, he had his business headquarters, run by a general manager with the assistance of two cashiers, five bookkeepers, and ten clerks. . . . On still another island was a sort of palace, where he lived in barbaric splendor with only his sister for company, and on still another was his harem. . . .[1]

Slaves were brought to Don Pedro's enormous compound at Lomboko after being captured by African tribes. There, they waited for a ship that would carry them on the long journey to plantations in the Americas.

The Voyage to Havana

Along with five hundred other Africans, Cinqué was led on board a Portuguese ship named the *Tecora* to begin a journey that would take approximately two months. The men were chained together and spent most of the voyage below deck, cramped into an area barely four feet high. They could not even stand up. The women and children were confined separately.

During the period of the Atlantic slave trade, historians estimate that as many as 10 to 20 million Africans were forced to make a similar journey.[2] One man, named Olaudah Equiano, described the terrible experience this way:

Joseph Cinqué and the other slaves on the Tecora *were chained and crowded like the slaves in this picture.*

> The closeness of the place, and the heat of the climate, added to the number in the ship, which was so crowded that each had scarcely room to turn himself, almost suffocated us. . . . the air soon became unfit for respiration, from a variety of loathsome smells, and brought on a sickness among the slaves, of which many died. . . .[3]

As the *Tecora* approached the Spanish-owned island of Cuba, the conditions of the African captives improved. Because they would need to appear healthy to fetch a good price in the Havana slave markets, Cinqué and the others were brought up on deck for longer periods. Here, they were unchained, dressed in clean clothes, and given better food to eat. Instead of sailing into Havana harbor with its cargo, the *Tecora* remained offshore. Under cover of night, the African captives were loaded into small boats and taken to Cuba. Then they marched inland where they remained in barracoons before going to the auction block.

All this secrecy was necessary because Spain and England had agreed to work together to outlaw the slave trade. Bringing slaves into the Spanish colony of Cuba was, therefore, illegal. The slave traders could lose their heads if they were caught. However, there was no law preventing Africans who were already slaves on the island of Cuba from being sold by one owner to another at auction. Thus, Cinqué and the other captives were smuggled onto the island, kept in confinement, then sold in Havana's slave mart as if they had always been slaves.

Aboard the *Amistad*

In June 1839, Cinqué was purchased in Havana by José Ruiz, who also bought forty-eight other slaves at a price of $450 each. His associate Pedro Montes purchased four children—three girls and a boy—from the same ship. By bribing government officials in Havana, Montes and Ruiz received passports verifying that all fifty-three slaves had been Spanish residents of Cuba and could be moved to another part of the island.[4]

Ruiz and Montes then transported the slaves to the ship *Amistad*, which was under the command of Ramón Ferrer. With a crew of two sailors, a cook named Celistino, and a cabin boy named Antonio, the ship set sail for Puerto Príncipe on another part of the island. There, the Africans would go to work on a Cuban plantation, growing and harvesting sugarcane.

Although the Africans were not chained during the day, they received little food or water during the hot, three-hundred-mile trip along the Cuban coast. When one of them, Burnah, tried to get something more to drink, he was flogged. Cinqué began to worry that there would not be enough food for the captives to survive the trip. He tried to communicate with the cook through sign language, since Cinqué could not speak Spanish and Celistino could not understand any African dialect. The Spanish cook simply smiled and indicated that some of the captives would be killed and fed to the others. It was a cruel joke, but Cinqué did not realize that the cook was joking.

Cinqué was horrified. He decided that the time had come to take action. On June 30, as the *Amistad* made its way along the Cuban coast, he stole a nail from the ship's stores. That night, as the slaves lay in chains, Cinqué used the nail to unlock his manacles (shackles for the hands). Then he released the other captives. Together with another African named Grabeau, Cinqué led the men to the place where the ship's weapons were stored. They helped themselves to knives and hatchets, then stormed the main deck where the captain was sleeping. Before Ferrer had time to defend himself, he had been overpowered and killed. The former slaves also turned on Celistino and butchered him with their hatchets. Although the rest of the crew jumped overboard, Ruiz and Montes were captured. They decided to surrender. The *Amistad* now belonged to the Africans.

The Voyage of the *Amistad*

The Africans wanted to return home to Mende country. Cinqué reasoned that the best way to get home was to sail toward the rising sun—that is, to the east. Because neither he nor any of the other Africans knew how to sail the ship, Cinqué forced Montes to chart a course to Sierra Leone in Africa.

Cinqué started the revolt on Amistad *that led to the death of the captain of the ship and most of the crew. Ruiz and Montez were kept alive as prisoners.*

Montes, however, had other plans. While heading east during part of the day, Montes steered the ship northward toward the North American coast at night. He hoped that it would be spotted by English or American sailing vessels and rescued. Meanwhile, the *Amistad* was running desperately short of food and water. Some of the Africans became so thirsty that they began drinking medicines that were stored on board and died. The Africans on board the *Amistad* tried to hail passing ships. But the other ships' captains were usually scared off when they drew close and saw black men armed with knives and hatchets.

Gradually, the *Amistad* sailed northward on a zigzag course that roughly paralleled the North American coast. Word of this strange ship with its African crew began to reach harbors along the continent. In August 1839, the *Amistad* finally anchored off the coast of Long Island, New York. Cinqué did not know where he had stopped. But the men needed food desperately, so he and some of the others went ashore to find food and water. Although they frightened most of the residents who saw them, Cinqué and the others were able to buy some supplies with money they had found aboard the *Amistad*.

But the activities of Cinqué and his men had not gone unobserved. They encountered a small party led by Captain Henry Green, who had heard about the ship and hoped to capture it. Cinqué wanted them to take the *Amistad* back to Africa. Out at sea, an American patrol boat, the U.S.S. *Washington*, under the command of Lieutenant Thomas R. Gedney, had spotted the *Amistad*. The men of the *Washington* had seen the Africans onshore, where they appeared to be engaged in smuggling. Gedney sent a few armed sailors, led by D. D. Porter and Richard W. Meade, in a small boat to board the *Amistad*.

Reaching the ship, they encountered some of the Africans, who had not gone onshore. They were quickly disarmed. Then Meade and his men found Ruiz and Montes below decks. In broken English, Ruiz explained what had happened—or at least, his side of the story. He claimed that the Africans were slaves being legally transported in Cuba, when they had revolted and killed the captain of the ship. According to Ruiz, what they had done was nothing less than mutiny and murder.

While the Africans were being held on board the *Amistad*, some of the American sailors went to shore. There, they captured Cinqué and the rest of his men. When he was brought on board the ship, Cinqué broke free and jumped over the side of the boat. He was finally captured and imprisoned aboard the *Amistad*. As the leader of the other Africans, he tried to spark a revolt so they could return home. But Lieutenant Gedney quickly removed him to the *Washington*.

Gedney then had to decide what to do with the *Amistad* and the people on board. If the Africans were slaves, as Ruiz claimed, they would be worth some money. Gedney might be able to claim a substantial reward from the government for capturing them and

Source Document

. . . On coming along side [the Amistad] a number of negroes were discovered on her deck, and twenty or thirty more were on the beach—two white men came forward and claimed the protection of the officer. The schooner proved to be the "Amistad," . . . with 54 blacks and two passengers on board; the former, four nights after they were out, rose and murdered the captain and three of the crew; they then took possession of the vessel with the intention of returning to the coast of Africa. . . . [T]he vessel was steered by Pedro Montes for New Providence, the negroes being under the impression that she was steering for the coast of Africa. . . . The situation of the two whites was all this time truly deplorable, being treated with the greatest severity. . . . The negroes were found in communication with shore, where they laid in a fresh supply of water, and were on the point of sailing again for the coast of Africa. They had a good supply of money with them, some of which it is likely was taken by the people on the beach.—After they were disarmed, and sent on board from the beach, the ringleader jumped overboard with three hundred doubloons about him, the property of the captain, all of which he succeeded in loosing from his person and then permitted himself to be captured.[5]

This account of the Amistad *revolt appeared in the* New London Gazette *on August 26, 1839.*

the ship. In New York, however, slavery was illegal, so his claim might not be allowed. In nearby Connecticut, however, slavery was still legal. Perhaps this is what persuaded Gedney to bring the ship to New London, Connecticut, on August 27, 1839.

The Importance of the *Amistad*

The capture of the *Amistad* may have seemed like a routine action by an American naval vessel. But it would rapidly become much more. The cause of Cinqué and the other Africans would quickly be taken up by the abolitionists, who wanted to bring an end to slavery throughout the United States. A series of celebrated court cases would result, ending in a landmark judgment by the United States Supreme Court. The *Amistad* case would help polarize feelings between the free states of the North and the slaveholding states of the South. The incident would not bring any resolution to the issue of slavery or the slave trade. Instead, it would serve as an important link in the chain of events that would eventually lead to the American Civil War.

Chapter 2

The Middle Passage

When Cinqué was captured near his village and clapped into slavery, he fell victim to a practice that was almost as old as civilization itself. Slaves had hoisted the giant stones in place to create the great pyramids of ancient Egypt. They had also built the impressive public monuments of ancient Greece and Rome. Slavery was accepted as an institution in the ancient world. Roman generals, for example, enslaved the people they conquered and brought their kings back to Rome in chains. "[A] slave is a living possession," wrote the Greek philosopher Aristotle.[1] Indeed, slaves were seen everywhere—working on large farms, making manufactured items in towns and cities, and rowing the giant galleys (ships) that sailed on the Mediterranean Sea.

After the fall of Rome in the fifth century, slavery continued. In wars between tribes, there were winners

Slavery existed long before the Americas were colonized. In ancient times, people like the Assyrians shown here were enslaved after being conquered.

and losers, conquerors and slaves. These slaves were sold at giant markets in European cities such as Verdun, Arles, and Lyons. Meanwhile, in North Africa, Muslim armies began to sweep across the continent. Although the Koran, or Muslim holy book, expressly forbade enslaving fellow Muslims, it did not prevent making slaves of infidels, or non-Muslims. In the eighth century, Arab soldiers crossed the Mediterranean Sea into Spain. They defeated the Visigoths who lived there, and these people became slaves of the Muslims.

The Arabs also extended their power southward from the Sahara Desert into central Africa. They came into contact with black African tribes, whose culture they regarded as inferior to their own. The Muslims made slaves of some of these people. Then they brought them to North Africa to dig in copper mines or to work sugarcane plantations.

During the thirteenth century, explained historian Hugh Thomas, "Moorish traders were to be found offering black slaves from Guinea [in Africa] at fairs . . . in northern Portugal; and blacks bought in North Africa were being sold in Cadiz [Spain] at the end of that century."[2] Thus, the Muslims extended black slavery to Spain and Portugal.

The Portuguese Explore the Atlantic

By this period, however, Arab influence on the Spanish peninsula was in decline. Throughout the Middle Ages, Christian kings had gradually driven

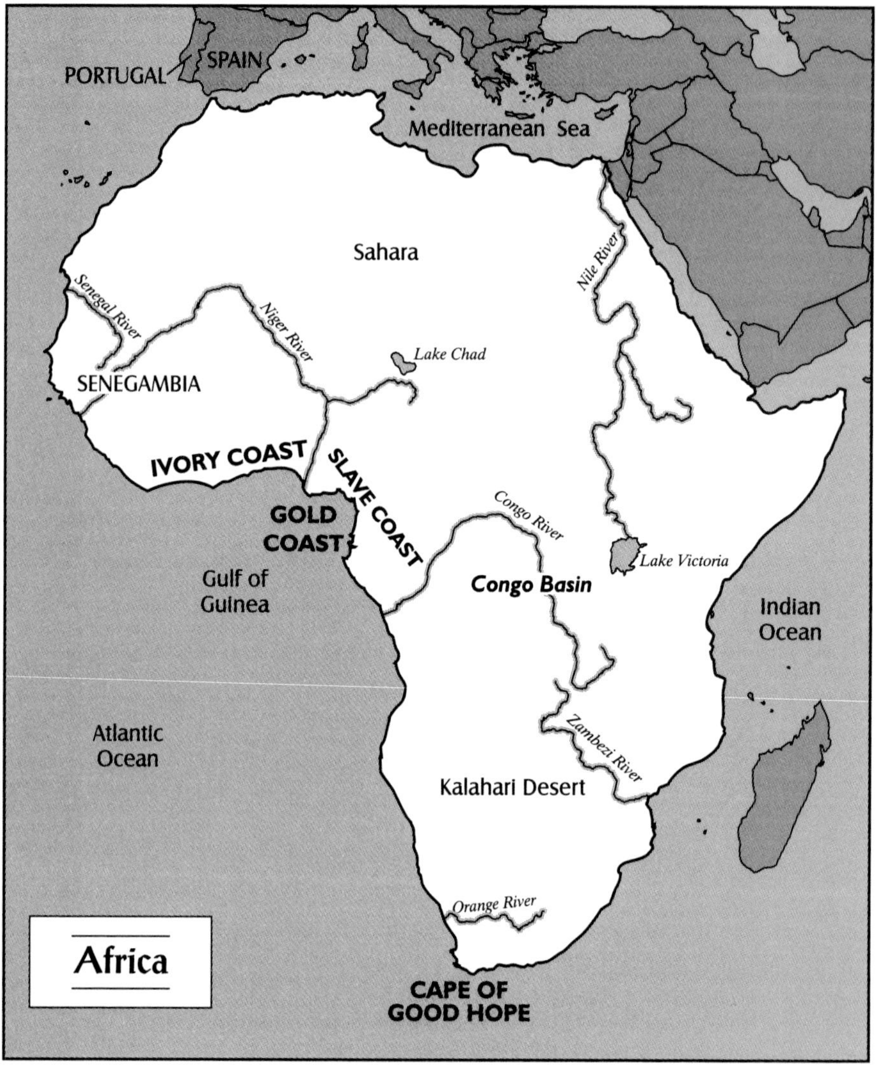

The African slave trade was mainly centered on the west coast of Africa, in the areas of the Gold Coast and Ivory Coast, which were often called the Slave Coast.

back the Moorish (Arab) invaders. By the fifteenth century, Arabs occupied only a small area in the southern part of Spain. Meanwhile, the power of the Portuguese and Spanish rulers had increased.

Portuguese explorers, under the direction of Prince Henry the Navigator, sailed southward along the African coast. They hoped to discover new sources of gold rumored to lie somewhere in the interior. The Portuguese landed at the mouth of the Senegal River, established settlements in the area that became known as Sierra Leone, and eventually reached the Benin and Congo rivers. However, they encountered powerful African empires that prevented them from penetrating very far inland. Disease and fear of the unknown also kept the Portuguese along the coast. There, they traded with the African empires for ivory, pepper, and gold. Beginning in the mid-fifteenth century, the Portuguese also began trading in something else, which they considered just as valuable as gold itself—black gold, or slaves.

Slavery had existed in Africa long before the arrival of the Portuguese. Prisoners taken in the tribal wars on the continent were often sold as slaves at huge fairs in what is now Senegal and Gambia in west Africa. But slavery at that time did not mean that a person was forced into a harsh, brutalized existence. "With us," wrote Olaudah Equiano, "they do no more work than other members of the community, even their masters; their food, clothing and lodging were nearly the same as theirs. . . . Some of these slaves have even slaves under them as their own property, and for their own use."[3]

As Portuguese traders arrived on the scene, the nature of slavery gradually changed. The Portuguese had already enslaved Moorish soldiers as they had been driven off the Spanish peninsula. Now they acquired African slaves—first by the hundreds, then by the thousands, and finally, by the tens of thousands. Some of these African slaves went to work in the households of wealthy families in Portugal. There, owning a slave came to be considered a symbol of wealth. But many other slaves were taken to the sugar plantations in southern Portugal, on the island of Madeira in the Atlantic Ocean, and at São Tomé in the Gulf of Guinea. Here, they were forced to do backbreaking labor, often for long hours each day. Slaves were no longer treated in the way that Olaudah Equiano described. Instead, they became property to be used in any way their masters wished.

To acquire these slaves, the Portuguese ships brought with them trade goods from Europe. These found a ready market among the African tribes. Trade goods included fine cloth from the Netherlands, brass bracelets from Germany, glass beads from Italy, knives and swords from Spain, and wine from the Canary Islands.[4] A lucrative trade developed, enriching merchants in many parts of Europe.

The Atlantic Slave Trade Begins

While the Portuguese developed their trade empire along the African coast, Spain was establishing its own empire in the Americas. Christopher Columbus planted the Spanish flag in the Caribbean Sea on islands that included Hispaniola and Cuba. A few years later, conquistadors such as Hernán Cortés and Francisco Pizarro added vast regions to the territory claimed by the Spanish Crown in Mexico and Peru. As Spanish settlers went to live in the New World, they tried to force the native American Indian populations into service on their plantations and *haciendas*, or

Columbus's discovery of islands in the Caribbean Sea spread slavery to the Americas.

large estates. But the Indians were indifferent workers. They were also exposed to fatal diseases, such as smallpox, which the Spanish brought with them. The Indians had no immunity to these diseases, and they died by the thousands.

Therefore, Spain still needed a large supply of new workers for its American colonies. Laborers were needed not only to plant sugarcane on the large plantations being staked out in South America, but also to dig for gold and silver in mines. In 1510, African slaves began arriving in Spain's American empire. Meanwhile, they were also being transported to the Portuguese colony of Brazil to work the huge sugar plantations there. During the sixteenth century, the demand for slaves grew until it seemed as if the

The Spanish and Portuguese went to Africa to buy slaves to work in the sugarcane fields of America.

Spanish and Portuguese colonies could not exist without them.

But no matter how many slaves arrived in the Americas, there never seemed to be enough of them to work the growing number of plantations. As a Spanish official in Lima, Peru, said in 1646: "The shortage of blacks threatens the total ruin of the entire kingdom, for the black slave is the basis of the hacienda and the source of all wealth which this realm produces."[5]

During this same period—from 1625 to 1650—approximately two hundred thousand slaves were imported to the Americas.[6] The life they were forced to lead was extremely harsh. Africans were routinely beaten by overseers and forced to work almost around the clock during the long sugarcane harvests. From the fields, the slaves transported the cane to sugar mills. There, the juice was ground out of the cane, boiled, skimmed, and cooled into rough sugar crystals. In the process, many slaves lost limbs in the machinery of the mill. Slaves were not expected to live long under the brutal conditions of the sugarcane plantations. Therefore, a fresh supply of slaves was constantly needed.

From the Americas, the rough sugar was transported to Europe, where it was refined. As the population of Europe grew, the demand increased for sugar to be used as a sweetener for tea, coffee, and milk, or as an ingredient in chocolate and other candy. Thus, a triangular trade developed. European ships brought trade goods to Africa in return for slaves.

Then the slaves were transported to the Americas to work on the sugar plantations. From there, raw sugar was carried back to Europe to be refined and used as a sweetener.

The Slave Trade Grows

Portugal and Spain were not the only countries with colonies in the Americas. Great Britain and France also established empires that demanded slaves. During the seventeenth and eighteenth centuries, British and French merchants supplied these slaves from trading posts in west Africa. These were located along the Ivory Coast, which was a rich source of ivory tusks, and the Gold Coast, an area with large gold deposits. The British referred to this entire area as Guinea. Some of the gold brought back to England was minted into coins, which were known as *guineas*.

But it was black gold—slaves—that made up the largest percentage of cargo brought out of Africa. British ships from Liverpool, Bristol, and London carried more than two hundred thousand slaves to the Americas between 1740 and 1750. Many of them worked the sugar plantations on the Caribbean islands of Jamaica and Barbados. Meanwhile, the Portuguese, Spanish, and French were also bringing slaves to their colonies. By the end of the eighteenth century, the total number of slaves leaving Africa each year reached eighty thousand.[7]

In return for these slaves, the English and other traders exchanged a vast assortment of goods with

African tribal chiefs. In addition to cloth and brass items, the chiefs were now interested in muskets to defend their lands as well as iron bars that could be melted down and shaped into farm tools. But to obtain these things, they had to supply an ever-increasing number of slaves to fill the demands of the European traders.

How the Slaves Were Supplied

Cinqué's long ordeal began when he was kidnapped by African slave traders near his village. Kidnapping was a primary method of supplying the large numbers of slaves requested by European merchants. In some cases, the victim may have owed a debt he could not pay. This may have been the reason Cinqué was taken.

Between 1740 and 1750, British ships brought thousands of slaves to work on Caribbean islands such as Jamaica.

Source Document

I was born in Dukandarra, in Guinea, about the year 1729. . . . A detachment from the enemy came to my father and informed him, that the whole army was encamped not far out of his dominions, and would invade the territory and deprive his people of their liberties and rights, if he did not comply with the following terms. These were to pay them a large sum of money, three hundred fat cattle, and a great number of goats, sheep, asses, etc.

My father told the messenger he would comply rather than that his subjects should be deprived of their rights and privileges. . . . We left our dwellings in succession, and my father's company went on first. We directed our course for a large shrub plain, some distance off, where we intended to conceal ourselves from the approaching enemy. . . . [The enemy] then came to us in the reeds, and the very first salute I had from them was a violent blow on the back part of the head with the fore part of a gun, and at the same time a grasp round the neck. I then had a rope put about my neck, as had all the women in the thicket with me, and were immediately led to my father, who was likewise pinioned and haltered for leading. . . . On a certain time I and other prisoners were put on board a canoe, under our master, and rowed away to a vessel belonging to Rhode Island, commanded by Captain Collingwood, and the mate Thomas Mumford. While we were going to the vessel, our master told us all to appear to the best possible advantage for sale.[8]

Venture Smith gave this account of his kidnapping into slavery at the age of six.

Others were enslaved as punishment for a crime, such as adultery, murder, or repeated thefts. Still others sold their children into slavery because they could not afford to feed them. Warfare also served as an important means of acquiring slaves. Indeed, some tribes may have initiated wars in order to capture their enemies so that they could be sold on the coast to the slave merchants.

Once a man like Cinqué was captured, he might begin a long trek before arriving at one of the European trading posts on the African coast. Cinqué, for example, was sold by his captors to a tribal prince, who then took him to the barracoon of Pedro Blanco. Other Africans reported being exchanged many times before reaching a ship bound for the Americas. Dr. Alexander Falconbridge, who was a surgeon aboard slave ships, reported being told by a black woman

> that as she was on her return home one evening, from some neighbors to whom she had been making a visit by invitation, she was kidnapped and notwithstanding she was big with child, she was sold for a slave. This transaction happened a considerable way up the country and she had passed through the hands of several purchasers before she reached the ship.[9]

Many slaves were sold at trade fairs. Black traders might set off from a European trading post on the coast with as many as twenty or thirty canoes. Each was large enough to carry up to forty slaves. The traders hoped to barter for them, according to Dr. Falconbridge, by putting

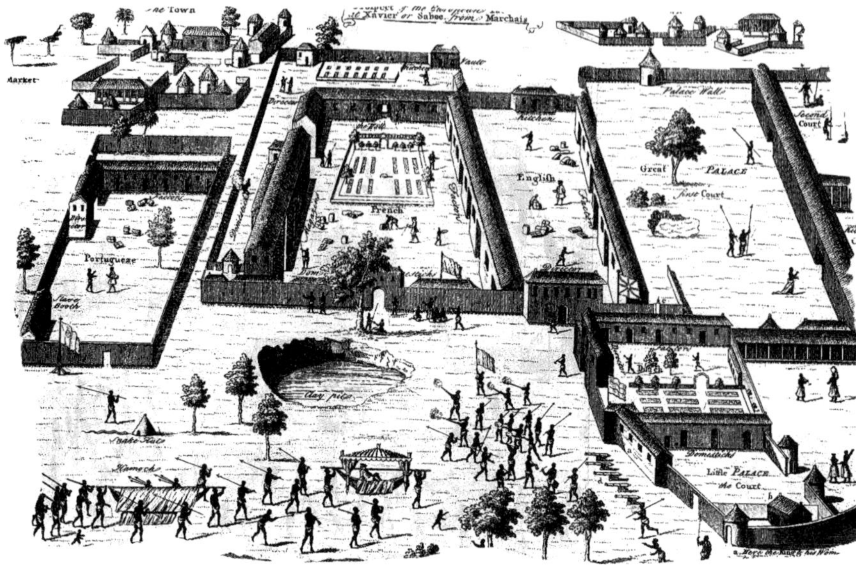

Several European countries set up slave trading facilities where slaves were kept and sold. These centers were often referred to as slave factories.

> such goods . . . on board as they expect will be wanted for the purchase of the number of slaves they intend to buy. When their loading is completed they commence their voyage with colors flying and music playing and in about ten or eleven days generally return . . . with full cargoes. As soon as the canoes arrive at the trader's landing place, the [slaves] are cleaned and oiled with palm oil and on the following day they are exposed for sale to the [ship] captains.[11]

Sometimes no ships were docked in port, and the slaves had to be housed in a barracoon. Cinqué was confined at Pedro Blanco's fort in Lomboko. It was a stout fortress with high towers, small huts for Blanco's

Source Document

Those sold by the Blacks are for the most part prisoners of war, taken either in fight, or pursuit, or in the incursions they make into their enemies territories; others stolen away by their own countrymen; and some there are, who will sell their own children, kindred, or neighbours. . . . The kings are so absolute, that upon any slight pretense of offences committed by their subjects, they order them to be sold for slaves, without regard to rank, or possession. . . . Abundance of little Blacks of both sexes are also stolen away by their neighbours, when found abroad on the roads, or in the woods. . . . In times of dearth and famine, abundance of those people will sell themselves, for a maintenance, and to prevent starving. . . .

Th[e] barbarous usage of those unfortunate wretches, makes it appear, that the fate of such as are bought and transported from the coast to America, or other parts of the world, by Europeans, is less deplorable, than that of those who end their days in their native country; for aboard ships all possible care is taken to preserve and subsist them for the interest of the owners, and when sold in America, the same motive ought to prevail with their masters to use them well, that they may live the longer, and do them more service.[10]

John Barbot, who worked for the French Royal African Company, described the slave trade in Africa in 1682.

men, and a large home for the trader. Cinqué was kept in a wooden building with the other slaves awaiting shipment to America.

Other barracoons were different. At the British fortress of Cabo Corso Castle on the Gold Coast, for example, slaves were kept in stone vaults below the ground. The only air came through an iron grating on the surface. As many as a thousand slaves might be kept below ground, chained together, before being put on board a ship. As they awaited transport, slaves might easily contract a disease and die.

Once the ships arrived, the next stage of the slaves' ordeal began. Before any was purchased, each would be carefully examined by a surgeon, such as Dr. Falconbridge. For this examination, the Africans would be stripped naked. The surgeon would test their limbs, examine their genitals for any disease, look into their eyes, and open their mouths to make sure their teeth were not rotten.

Once the slaves were purchased, another ritual occurred. As one slave captain explained:

> Then we mark'd the slaves we had bought in the breast, or shoulder, with a hot iron, having the letter of the ship's name on it, the place being before anointed with a little palm oil, which caused but little pain, the mark being usually well in four or five days, appearing very plain and white after.[12]

The slaves, who had been branded like horses or cattle, were then loaded aboard ship to begin the next leg of their long journey.

The Middle Passage

For Africans like Cinqué, the most difficult part of their journey may have occurred as their ship began to pull away from the African coast. Cinqué realized that he would probably never see his home or his wife and three children again. For some of the captives, this terrible realization was too much to bear. They threw themselves overboard into the harbor, where they were often eaten alive by sharks. Apparently, even a terrible death seemed better than being separated from home and family. Since they had no idea where they were going or what terrible things might happen to them, they committed suicide rather than face the horrors of the unknown.

The rest of the captives, however, began a long voyage to the Americas. The trip to America was called the Middle Passage—the middle part of the triangular trade. In good weather, this trip might last from thirty to fifty days. The voyage was much longer if the ship encountered storms crossing the Atlantic. Because the Africans had never been to sea, they usually became violently seasick. Their misery was made even worse by the terrible conditions in which they were forced to live during the voyage. Cinqué was one of five hundred slaves crammed below decks in the ship *Tecora*. All the men were chained together in a small area where it was impossible for them to stand up. There was very little fresh air, except for the breezes that might come through the portholes.

Dr. Falconbridge explained how such conditions often affected the slaves:

> During the voyages I made, I was frequently witness to the fatal effects of this exclusion of fresh air. . . . Some wet and blowing weather having occasioned the port-holes to be shut and the grating to be covered, fluxes and fevers among the Negroes ensued. While they were in this situation, I frequently went down among them till at length their room became so extremely hot as to be only bearable for a very short time. . . . The deck, that is the floor of their rooms, was so covered with the blood and mucus which had proceeded from them in consequence of . . . [sickness], that it resembled a slaughter-house.[13]

Since the slavers got paid by the head, it was in their best interests to deliver as many people as possible to the Americas. Nevertheless, many Africans died from diseases such as dysentery, smallpox, and dehydration. Not only the captives, but also the crews of the slave ships often complained of too little water. "Much of what there was became foul during the course of the voyage, growing thick with algae," explained historian Madeleine Burnside. "Only recently has dehydration been understood as the underlying medical cause of the depression so often noted in the African captives."[14]

The captives were not kept below deck all the time. The men were brought on the top deck two or three times a day to be fed. However, they were securely chained together to prevent mutinies. Women and children were kept separate from the men. Unlike the male slaves, they were not chained because they posed less of a threat to the crew of the slave ship.

Even with these precautions, rebellions did occur. But they were usually put down by the heavily armed crew. Sometimes the leaders of the rebellion would jump overboard and face drowning rather than the punishment that awaited them. Frequently, Burnside

Source Document

About one in the afternoon, after dinner, we, according to custom caused them, one by one, to go down between decks, to have each his pint of water; most of them were yet above deck, many of them provided with knives, which we had indiscreetly given them two or three days before, as not suspecting the least attempt of this nature from them; others had pieces of iron they had torn off our forecastle door. . . . Thus arm'd, they fell in crouds and parcels on our men, upon the deck unawares, and stabb'd one of the stoutest of us all, who receiv'd fourteen or fifteen wounds of their knives, and so expir'd. . . . [W]e stood in arms, firing on the revolted slaves, of whom we kill'd some, and wounded many: which so terrif'd the rest, that they gave way, dispersing themselves some one way and some another between decks, and under the forecastle; and many of the most mutinous, leapt over board, and drown'd themselves in the ocean. . . .[15]

James Barbot, Jr., a sailor aboard the English slave ship Don Carlos, *gave this account of a slave uprising that took place aboard the vessel in 1700.*

wrote, "the participating slaves were flogged and their leaders killed. Many slave ship captains also believed it prudent to dismember publicly the leaders of a revolt, letting their fate serve as a warning to the others."[16] In one case, the leader of a revolt had his right hand cut off, then his left, and finally, he was beheaded.

Slave ships headed for the Americas might put in at one of the ports where large slave auctions were held. These might include Rio de Janeiro, Brazil; Cartagena, on the northern coast of South America; or Havana, Cuba. From these slave marts the slaves were transported to plantations to spend the rest of their lives under the whip of a harsh overseer.

Life on a Cuban Plantation

Cuba was a lush, tropical island crisscrossed with huge sugar and coffee plantations. No other island in the Caribbean grew as many tons of sugar each year as this small Spanish colony. What made the enormous sugar-cane crop possible, however, were thousands and thousands of slaves. As one Spanish governor-general on the island put it, "if there is no slave labor, the island's wealth will disappear within a few years. . . ."[17]

As a slave on a Cuban plantation, Cinqué's life would no longer be his own. He would become a piece of property that could be ordered to do anything by his master, sold whenever his master wanted, and severely punished if he should ever disobey. James Thompson was owned by several masters before becoming a field worker and a house servant on a coffee plantation.

He recalled that, each day, the old mistress of the plantation would come into the kitchen and "strike me with a stick for some real or imaginary fault. . . ." She was never satisfied with him, although he not only cooked for the family, but after his household duties were done, he also picked coffee in the fields. After she died, his situation grew even worse:

> Her son and daughter continually ill-used me; the latter would frequently take a stick out of the fire, and break it over my head; and the former one day gave me such a severe beating with his *manati* (a whip made of the skin of the sea-cow) that I was three days in the hospital.

While he worked on the plantation, Thompson fell in love with a woman and asked for permission to marry her. Slaves were not allowed to marry without the consent of their masters. But permission was refused. Instead, Thompson and his girlfriend were placed side by side on the ground and each given two hundred fifty lashes:

> After this, we had irons placed on our feet, with a chain connecting them suspended from the waist. A collar with three hooks was placed round our necks and a coupling chain secured to each collar. Thus linked together, we worked in the field for two years and a half, being every night and during the hours of rest on the Sundays and festivals, confined in the stocks.[18]

A similar fate most likely awaited Cinqué, unless he could escape.

Chapter 3

The *Amistad* and American Slavery

In order to have a steady supply of slaves available, plantation owners in Cuba relied on the Atlantic slave traders. But by 1839, the year Cinqué arrived in Cuba, this slave trade had become illegal. More than half a century earlier, reformers in England—a leader in the slave trade—began to agitate for an end to this terrible practice.

Efforts to End the Slave Trade

The reform movement was led by Thomas Clarkson, a founder of the Society for the Abolition of the Slave Trade. He published pamphlets based on the information he gathered from talking to seamen who were involved in the slave trade.

Another leader of the reform movement was brilliant politician William Wilberforce, whose stirring speeches in Parliament (the British legislature) condemned the work of the English merchants who had sold so many Africans into slavery. "Africa, Africa," Wilberforce said in one of his speeches, "your sufferings have been the theme that has arrested and engages my heart. Your sufferings no tongue can express, no language impart."[1]

At first, there was enormous opposition to ending the slave trade because so many merchants were growing rich from it. Still, the reformers persisted. Gradually, they won over public opinion by exposing the cruelties of slavery. In 1807, Parliament passed a law that outlawed the slave trade in the British colonies.

After passage of the law, English slave stations in Africa were abandoned, and the navy began to patrol the African coast to stop the flow of slaves to the Americas. The British realized, however, that it was not enough simply to eliminate the slave trade in their own empire; other nations had to do the same thing. Under pressure from England, whose powerful navy controlled the sea, Spain and Portugal decided to eliminate the slave trade, too. They also gave British ships the right to stop any Portuguese or Spanish vessels suspected of carrying slaves. Thus, the Portuguese ship *Tecora* was violating the law by bringing Cinqué and the other Africans to Cuba. The ship could have been stopped, its cargo confiscated, and its captain hauled into court in Cuba to stand trial for engaging in the slave trade.

Slave trading was a risky business. But the British and their allies had so few ships to patrol the waters that many slavers made it to Cuba without being caught. In 1836, just three years before Cinqué's arrival, sixty thousand slaves had been brought there.[2] Why did so many slave ships get through? As historian Warren Howard put it: "The fundamental answer is that none of the nations trying to suppress the trade was serious enough to employ adequate naval patrols. . . . [T]he much-publicized British African squadron never had half as many cruisers as it needed. . . ."[3] And in the Caribbean, Spain and Great Britain employed very few ships to stop the slavers.

Nevertheless, slave merchants did not flout the law too openly. Once they arrived off the island of Cuba, the slaves were taken on shore under cover of night. Then they were hidden in confinement areas for short periods before being taken to the Havana slave auctions. All this deception was to make it look as if the slaves were already employed at a coffee or sugar plantation and were simply being sold to another plantation owner. Although the international slave trade was illegal, slavery on the island of Cuba was perfectly legal, and slave trade on the island itself was protected by law.

Of course, the Spanish authorities were not really fooled. But they received large bribes to look the other way. Indeed, one governor-general was rumored to have put a half ounce of gold in his pocket every time a slave reached Cuba safely. As Nicholas Trist, the United States consul in Havana, explained in 1839,

> The truth of the existing state of things here, in relation to the slave-trade, can be condensed into one sentence. It is a pursuit denounced in every possible way by the LAW—by law FOREIGN made and FOREIGN imposed—and supported by an overwhelming PUBLIC OPINION. . . .[4]

Trist might have added that American merchants were also participating in the slave trade. The United States, unlike Spain and Portugal, had never given the British permission to stop and search its ships. Sleek merchant vessels, manufactured in American ports such as Baltimore, Maryland, were sent south to Havana. From there, they were used by Spanish and Portuguese slavers on their trips to Africa, often sailing with an American captain and under an American flag to elude the British patrols. Thus American businessmen, as well as their counterparts in Cuba, made huge profits from the slave trade. Some of these slaves were also being transported from Havana to the United States to work on the huge cotton plantations in the South.

Origins of Slavery in the South

The schooner *Amistad* that brought Cinqué and his companions to North America had originally been built in the Baltimore shipyards. But the ship was hardly being used for the purposes its builders had intended. As the *Amistad* zigzagged northward, reports of this strange ship reached the mainland, causing fear among Southerners who heard that blacks were in control of the ship. If this were true, it posed a threat to a Southern society that was based on the institution of black slavery.

African slavery had been introduced to the American colonies in 1619 when a Dutch ship arrived in Jamestown, Virginia, with twenty Africans to be sold as slaves. However, slavery grew slowly because Southern farm owners relied on indentured servants to help them work their land. These impoverished people sold their services for a fixed period of time, in return for passage to America and a place to live. As tobacco plantations developed in Virginia, Maryland, and North Carolina, indentured servants remained the primary labor force working the fields.

During the latter part of the seventeenth century, however, fewer of England's poor came to North America. Jobs were more plentiful at home. Gradually, Southern planters began to rely more heavily on black slaves to work the tobacco fields as well as the huge rice plantations that developed in North and South Carolina. At first, white and black field hands worked side by side. Many blacks were freed after a specific period of time, just like indentured servants. They then bought their own land, and generally enjoyed many of the same rights as white plantation owners.

The Nature of Slavery Changes

Over the next century, the demand for slaves on Southern plantations continued to grow. Many of these slaves were supplied by the Royal African Company, whose sailing ships transported them from Africa. American merchants also participated in the slave trade. Biographer Edward Ball described the activities of one of his ancestors, Henry Laurens—a co-owner of the Charleston, South Carolina, merchant firm of Austin and Laurens. "In the ten years between 1751 and 1761," Ball wrote, "George Austin and Henry Laurens brought sixty-one slave galleys to the Charleston wharfs—the largest number of any slave importer in the city. . . ."[5] Indeed, from the beginning of the eighteenth century, more than 40 percent of all the slaves arriving in North America came through Charleston.[6]

In the Southern states, the proportion of blacks in the population increased dramatically. Between 1680 and 1750, the number grew from 7 percent to 44 percent in Virginia, for example, and from 17 percent to 61 percent in South Carolina.[7] In the North, by contrast, there were never many slaves. Most Northerners owned small farms and grew only enough food to feed themselves. The Northern colonies did not develop huge tobacco and rice plantations, which needed large numbers of laborers. However, merchants in the North did not hesitate to participate in the slave trade, which offered huge profits for anyone willing to sail the Atlantic. Ship captains from ports such as Boston, Massachusetts; New London, Connecticut; and Newport, Rhode Island; regularly sailed to Africa with casks of rum manufactured in New England. They would trade this rum with African chiefs for slaves—two hundred gallons of rum per slave in the middle of the eighteenth century.[8] Then they would take the slaves to the Caribbean islands, where they would be sold. Part of the profit would be invested in molasses, which would be taken back to New England and used to make rum. In addition to this triangular trade, New England merchants also took lumber and fish to the West Indies, where they were sold for slaves who were then transported to the Southern colonies.

As the number of slaves in the South increased, the laws that governed them gradually became much harsher. Perhaps white Southerners grew worried about having such a large slave population in their midst—a population that looked different and had different customs. Slaves might revolt against their masters. A series of laws was enacted in the Southern states that institutionalized slavery and ensured that black slaves would remain in a subordinate position. Slaves were expected to remain in slavery for life and plantation owners were encouraged not to free them. In addition, slaves were not allowed to carry weapons or to leave the plantation without written permission. Any slaves who did not obey their masters could expect severe punishment.

Historian Peter Kolchin explained,

> Born in violence, slavery survived by the lash. Beginning with the initial slave trade that tore Africans away from everything they knew and sent them in chains to a distant land to toil for strangers, every stage of master-slave relations depended either directly or indirectly on physical coercion. The routine functioning of Southern farms and plantations rested on the authority of the owners . . . supported by the state, to inflict pain on their human property. Plenty of pain was inflicted.[9]

One slave named Madison Jefferson repeatedly tried to escape from the plantation where he worked. Once, when he was recaptured, his master told him that he would be brutally beaten. Jefferson received fifty lashes and was chained at night but was released to work in the fields during the day. Plantation workers on the large plantations were supervised by black slave drivers who operated under the direction of a white overseer, or the master himself on smaller plantations. Men and women who could not do their work were given twenty-five to thirty lashes over their clothes. If this did not convince them to work harder, the overseer would inflict another flogging of sixty to one hundred lashes. Even pregnant women were lashed, Jefferson recalled.[10]

From the Constitution to the Cotton Gin

In 1776, the American colonies declared their independence from Great Britain. Over the next few years, they fought a war to ensure their freedom. For many of the patriots, the notion of individual liberty seemed inconsistent with the practice of slavery. Following the American victory in the Revolutionary War, the Northern states gradually abolished slavery. In the South, however, slavery remained. It formed the bedrock of the plantation system.

At the Constitutional Convention of 1787, several Southern delegates threatened that their states would not join any new federal union if the slave trade were not protected. The Constitution does not mention slavery by name, but it does contain a compromise worked out by the Founding Fathers at the Constitutional Convention. It states that "the Migration or Importation of such Persons as any of the States now existing shall think proper to admit, shall not be prohibited by the Congress prior to the Year one thousand eight hundred and eight. . . ." This clause refers to the slave trade—that is, bringing slaves into the United States, which was not to be ended until 1808. The Constitution also protected slave owners whose slaves ran away. It stated that they will "be delivered up on Claim of the Party to whom such Service or Labour may be due."

Although Southern delegates made every effort to protect the institution of slavery, it was actually beginning to decline among the Southern states along the east coast. Tobacco growing had gradually exhausted the soil of the plantations. It was no longer as valuable a cash crop.

Then, in 1793, a young tutor named Eli Whitney invented a device that would enable slaves to separate more rapidly the fiber from the seed of short staple cotton. This was the only type of cotton that could flourish on plantations that were not located along the coast. The cotton gin, as the device was called, led directly to the development of cotton plantations in states such as Arkansas, Alabama, Mississippi, and Louisiana. In the past, it had taken a slave an entire day to clean a pound of cotton. With a hand cotton gin, a slave could clean fifty pounds of cotton a day; larger power-driven gins could clean a thousand pounds of cotton daily. From 138,000 pounds of cotton produced in the South in 1792, production rose to over 17 million pounds by 1800.[11] Eventually, cotton would become America's biggest export. The demand was greatest in England, where mills turned cotton into cloth. But New England mill owners also depended on Southern-grown cotton for the domestic cloth industry.

As cotton growing expanded, the demand for slaves began to grow again. In the three years before the abolition of the international slave trade in 1808, 202 vessels came into Charleston Harbor carrying slaves. After 1808, when the external slave trade was formally abolished in the United States, an illegal trade in slaves continued. Slaves were brought into the United States from Galveston Island in Texas, which was still part of Spanish Mexico. Another trading center was Amelia Island, off northern Florida. The

Eli Whitney's creation, the cotton gin, revived the need for slaves in the South.

pirates Jean and Pierre Lafitte sent their ships into the Caribbean from Barataria Bay, south of New Orleans, to hijack slave ships and bring their cargoes illegally into the United States. In 1820, the United States government strengthened the laws against the slave trade, making any violation punishable by death. As a result, the slave trade declined for a time, but increased again a decade later.

By far the largest slave trade took place within the South itself, where it was perfectly legal to buy and sell slaves. Plantation owners in the east no longer needed as many slaves because their soil was exhausted from growing tobacco. They found it very profitable to sell their slaves to planters farther west. As Edward Ball explained, his ancestors were no different. They found selling slaves at auction a profitable business: "It was not unusual in this period to see long columns of black people tramping in chains through the wilderness, on a forced march from South Carolina to the new cotton plantations. The Ball auction was nicely timed to meet the demand."[12]

Meanwhile, the population of Southern slaves was increasing due to the high birthrates among black women and a lower death rate. Slaves were probably treated somewhat better in the South than in the Caribbean or South America, and there were fewer diseases. In 1810, just after the end of the legal slave trade, the slave population stood at just over one million. By 1860, there were almost 4 million slaves.[13]

The cotton gin allowed slaves to clean fifty times more cotton than they could do by hand.

Along with Cuba and Brazil, the Southern states were virtually the only areas in the Western Hemisphere where slavery was still legal. Indeed, slavery was so much a part of the Southern economy and society that Southerners felt it was their duty to defend it against any and all threats.

The *Amistad* case posed such a threat. It would ignite a firestorm in the South.

Chapter 4

Igniting the Firestorm

For many years, New London, Connecticut, had been considered one of the principal seaports in the North. It was an important center of the whaling industry. During the eighteenth century, New London merchants had also grown rich from the far-flung triangular trade that had brought so many slaves to the Americas. When the *Amistad* was brought to New London in August 1839, following its capture by the U.S.S. *Washington*, slavery was still legal in Connecticut.

Shortly after the *Amistad* docked in New London, federal district Judge Andrew T. Judson was notified of the situation. On August 27, he held an inquiry aboard the U.S.S. *Washington* into the facts surrounding the mutiny on the *Amistad* that had led to the death of the captain and the cook. Judge Judson verified from the ship's papers that the *Amistad* had been involved in transporting slaves along the coast of Cuba. He also talked to José Ruiz and Pedro Montes, who claimed to own the slaves. And he interviewed Antonio—a black slave who had belonged to the ship's captain. All of them said that Cinqué had led an illegal mutiny. It appeared that the Africans were guilty of piracy and murder.

Ruiz and Montes asked that the *Amistad* be handed over to the Spanish authorities. But Judson did not want to make any decision too hastily. He ordered the Africans, thirty-nine adults and four children, to be held for a few weeks in a New Haven, Connecticut, jail. Then they would be taken before the grand jury of the United States circuit court, which was due to meet in Hartford, Connecticut. The grand jury would decide what should happen to them.

The *Amistad* case might have been quietly and quickly handled by the Hartford grand jury, without most people ever hearing about it—except for the presence of one man who had been aboard the *Washington*. His name was Dwight P. Janes, an abolitionist who lived in New London. In an off-the-record conversation with Ruiz, Janes had learned that none of the Africans was really a Cuban slave. They had been brought to the island illegally. This meant that they were free. Janes decided that he must do everything possible to help them regain their freedom. As a strong believer in abolition, he also hoped to turn the *Amistad* incident into a highly publicized event that might help abolish slavery.

The Rise of Abolition

The abolition movement had existed since the eighteenth century, especially among the Quakers of Pennsylvania. They strongly believed that slavery and the slave trade were morally wrong and should be stopped immediately. Following the American Revolution, most Northern states gradually abolished slavery, but the institution continued in the South. However, most Northerners felt that slavery should be left alone, not abolished by force. They expected that it would eventually die out as it was doing in the North.

Having little national support for abolition, antislavery advocates began to focus their attention on an alternative. They encouraged Southern planters to free their slaves one by one so the slaves could be resettled in Africa. In 1821, the American Colonization Society founded the territory of Liberia in west Africa. The colony began receiving black settlers a year later. Among the society's early supporters were a young journalist named William Lloyd Garrison and wealthy New York merchants Lewis and Arthur Tappan.

While Liberia was being established, a religious revival movement began to sweep through many parts of America. Religious leaders called on their followers to rededicate themselves to creating a society that would be free from sin and run according to high moral principles. They envisioned a nation that would eliminate the vices of gambling, drinking, adultery, and slavery—for slavery seemed completely opposed to all religious teachings. Men such as Garrison and the Tappan brothers began to realize that colonization would never free the slaves. Only abolition could be successful. In 1831, Garrison began publishing *The Liberator*, which became one of the most powerful abolitionist journals. Although its circulation was always small, its inflammatory language condemning slavery and the plantation system incensed Southerners.

In 1833, Great Britain abolished slavery throughout its colonies in the West Indies. That same year, Garrison, the Tappans, and almost sixty other abolitionists founded the American Anti-Slavery Society. Over the next few years, the society submitted petitions to Congress calling for the abolition of slavery. The society also began a direct mail campaign, sending literature to politicians, ministers, and editors in the North and South, calling for the slaves to be freed.

The South's Reaction

The South reacted furiously to efforts by the Anti-Slavery Society to promote abolition. On July 29, 1835, the people of Charleston, South Carolina, stormed the post office and removed the mail so no abolitionist literature could be distributed. They also burned effigies, or images, of William Lloyd Garrison and Arthur Tappan. Southerners believed that the abolitionists were interfering with something that was none of their business, undermining the foundations of the South's economy.

William Lloyd Garrison published The Liberator*, an abolitionist journal. He was blamed for inciting slave uprisings.*

Plantation owners were already nervous about keeping their slaves under control. Escape attempts were frequent. Historians have estimated that fifty thousand slaves tried to get away each year.[1] Armed patrols regularly roamed the roads, looking for escaped slaves. Slave revolts posed a constant threat to Southerners. They feared that, at any moment, an army of slaves might march down the road to attack their homes—burning, looting, and pillaging.

Rebellions had already occurred a number of times in the past. Along the Stono River near Charleston, a slave named Cato led a small revolt in 1739 that became known as the Stono Rebellion. The slaves attacked a storehouse containing arms and ammunition, then headed south toward Florida, gathering followers as they marched. Once the white militia turned out, however, it was able to corner Cato. After a bloody battle, most of the slaves were captured and executed.

In 1791, Southern planters reacted with horror to a massive slave uprising in the French colony of Saint-Domingue (Haiti) on the island of Hispaniola in the Caribbean Sea. The hero of that revolution was a free black man named Toussaint L'Ouverture, who conquered the rest of Hispaniola, freed the slaves there, and established an independent government.

Slave Rebellions in the United States

Southerners feared the same thing might happen to them. Although they tried to keep their slaves illiterate, some slaves read about L'Ouverture's exploits. One of

THE LIBERATOR.

VOL. I.] WILLIAM LLOYD GARRISON AND ISAAC KNAPP, PUBLISHERS. [NO. 1.

BOSTON, MASSACHUSETTS.] OUR COUNTRY IS THE WORLD—OUR COUNTRYMEN ARE MANKIND. [SATURDAY, JANUARY 1, 1831.

THE LIBERATOR
IS PUBLISHED WEEKLY
AT NO. 6, MERCHANTS' HALL.

WM. L. GARRISON, EDITOR.
Stephen Foster, Printer.

TERMS.

☞ Two Dollars per annum, payable in advance.

☞ Agents allowed every sixth copy gratis.

☞ No subscription will be received for a shorter period than six months.

☞ All letters and communications must be POST PAID.

THE LIBERATOR.

To date my being from the opening year,
I come, a stranger in this busy sphere,
Where some I meet perchance may pause and ask,
What is my name, my purpose, or my task?

My name is 'LIBERATOR'! I propose
To hurl my shafts at freedom's deadliest foes!
My task is hard—for I am charged to save
Man from his brother!—to redeem the slave!

Ye who may hear, and yet condemn my cause,
Say, shall the best of Nature's holy laws
Be trodden down? and shall her open veins
Flow but for cement to her offspring's chains?

Art thou a parent? shall thy children be
Rent from thy breast, like branches from the tree,
And doom'd to servitude, in helplessness,
On other shores, and thou ask no redress?

Thou, in whose bosom glows the sacred flame
Of filial love, say, if the tyrant came,
To force thy parent shrieking from thy sight,
Would thy heart bleed—because thy face is white?

Art thou a brother? shall thy sister twine
Her feeble arm in agony on thine,
And thou not lift the heel, nor aim the blow
At him who bears her off to life-long woe?

Art thou a sister? will no desp'rate cry
Awake thy sleeping brother, while thine eye
Beholds the fetters locking on the limb
Stretched out in rest, which hence, must end for him?

Art thou a lover?—no! naught e'er was found
In lover's breast, save cords of love, that bound
Man to his kind! then, thy professions save!
Forswear affection, or release thy slave!

Thou who art kneeling at thy Maker's shrine,
Ask if Heaven takes such offerings as thine!
If in thy bonds the son of Afric sighs,
Far higher than thy prayer his groan will rise!

God is a God of mercy, and would see
The prison-doors unbarr'd—the bondmen free!
He is a God of truth, with purer eyes
Than to behold the oppressor's sacrifice!

Avarice, thy cry and thine insatiate thirst
Make man consent to see his brother cursed!
Tears, sweat and blood thou drink'st, but in their turn,
They shall cry 'more!' while vengeance bids thee burn.

The Lord hath said it!—who shall him gainsay?
He says, 'the wicked, they shall go away'—
Who are the wicked?——Contradict who can,
They are the oppressors of their fellow man!

Aid me, NEW ENGLAND! 'tis my hope in you
Which gives me strength my purpose to pursue!
Do you not hear your sister States resound
With Afric's cries to have her sons unbound?

TO THE PUBLIC.

In the month of August, I issued proposals for publishing 'THE LIBERATOR' in Washington city; but the enterprise, though hailed in different sections of the country, was palsied by public indifference. Since that time, the removal of the *Genius of Universal Emancipation* to the Seat of Government has rendered less imperious the establishment of a similar periodical in that quarter.

During my recent tour for the purpose of exciting the minds of the people by a series of discourses on the subject of slavery, every place that I visited gave fresh evidence of the fact, that a greater revolution in public sentiment was to be effected in the free states—and *particularly* in *New-England*—than at the south. I found contempt more bitter, opposition more active, detraction more relentless, prejudice more stubborn, and apathy more frozen, than among slave owners themselves. Of course, there were individual exceptions to the contrary. This state of things afflicted, but did not dishearten me. I determined, at every hazard, to lift up the standard of emancipation in the eyes of the nation, *within sight of Bunker Hill and in the birth place of liberty.* That standard is now unfurled; and long may it float, unhurt by the spoliations of time or the missiles of a desperate foe—yea, till every chain be broken, and every bondman set free! Let southern oppressors tremble—let their secret abettors tremble—let their northern apologists tremble—let all the enemies of the persecuted blacks tremble.

I deem the publication of my original Prospectus unnecessary, as it has obtained a wide circulation. The principles therein inculcated will be steadily pursued in this paper, excepting that I shall not array myself as the political partisan of any man. In defending the great cause of human rights, I wish to derive the assistance of all religions and of all parties.

Assenting to the 'self-evident truth' maintained in the American Declaration of Independence, 'that all men are created equal, and endowed by their Creator with certain inalienable rights—among which are life, liberty and the pursuit of happiness,' I shall strenuously contend for the immediate enfranchisement of our slave population. In Park-street Church, on the Fourth of July, 1829, in an address on slavery, I unreflectingly assented to the popular but pernicious doctrine of *gradual* abolition. I seize this opportunity to make a full and unequivocal recantation, and thus publicly to ask pardon of my God, of my country, and of my brethren the poor slaves, for having uttered a sentiment so full of timidity, injustice and absurdity. A similar recantation, from my pen, was published in the Genius of Universal Emancipation at Baltimore, in September, 1829. My conscience is now satisfied.

I am aware, that many object to the severity of my language; but is there not cause for severity? I *will be* as harsh as truth, and as uncompromising as justice. On this subject, I do not wish to think, or speak, or write, with moderation. No! no! Tell a man whose house is on fire, to give a moderate alarm; tell him to moderately rescue his wife from the hands of the ravisher; tell the mother to gradually extricate her babe from the fire into which it has fallen;—but urge me not to use moderation in a cause like the present. I am in earnest—I will not equivocate—I will not excuse—I will not retreat a single inch—AND I WILL BE HEARD. The apathy of the people is enough to make every statue leap from its pedestal, and to hasten the resurrection of the dead.

It is pretended, that I am retarding the cause of emancipation by the coarseness of my invective, and the precipitancy of my measures. *The charge is not true.* On this question my influence,—humble as it is,—is felt at this moment to a considerable extent, and shall be felt in coming years—not perniciously, but beneficially—not as a curse, but as a blessing; and posterity will bear testimony that I was right. I desire to thank God, that he enables me to disregard 'the fear of man which bringeth a snare,' and to speak his truth in its simplicity and power. And here I close with this fresh dedication:

'Oppression! I have seen thee, face to face,
And met thy cruel eye and cloudy brow;
But thy soul-withering glance I fear not now—
For dread to prouder feelings doth give place
Of deep abhorrence! Scorning the disgrace
Of slavish knees that at thy footstool bow,
I also kneel—but with far other vow
Do hail thee and thy herd of hirelings base:—
I swear, while life-blood warms my throbbing veins,
Still to oppose and thwart, with heart and hand,
Thy brutalising sway—till Afric's chains
Are burst, and Freedom rules the rescued land,—
Trampling Oppression and his iron rod:
Such is the vow I take—SO HELP ME GOD!'

WILLIAM LLOYD GARRISON.
BOSTON, January 1, 1831.

*I would here offer my grateful acknowledgments to those editors who so promptly and generously inserted my Proposals. They must give me an available opportunity to repay their liberality.

DISTRICT OF COLUMBIA.

What do many of the professed enemies of slavery mean, by heaping all their reproaches upon the south, and assailing nothing but the crime of oppression as not national? What power but Congress—and Congress by the authority of the American people—has jurisdiction over the District of Columbia? That [illegible] stinks in the nostrils of the world. Though it be the seat of the National Government,—open to the daily inspection of foreign ambassadors,—and ostensibly opulent with the congregated wisdom, virtue and intelligence of the land,—yet a fouler spot scarcely exists on earth. In it the worst features of slavery are exhibited; and as a mart for slave traders, it is unequalled. These facts are well known to our two or three hundred representatives, but no remedy is proposed; they are known, if not minutely at least generally, to our whole population,—but who calls for redress?

Hitherto, a few straggling petitions, relative to this subject, have gone into Congress; but they have been too few to denote much public anxiety, or to command a deferential notice. It is certainly time that a vigorous and systematic effort should be made, from one end of the country to the other, to pull down that national monument of oppression which towers up in the District. We do hope that the 'earthquake voice' of the people will this session shake the black fabric to its foundation.

The following petition is now circulating in this city, and has obtained several valuable signatures. A copy may be found at the Bookstore of LINCOLN & EDMANDS, No. 59, Washington-street, for a few days longer, where all the friends of the cause are earnestly invited to go and subscribe.

Petition to Congress for the Abolition of Slavery in the District of Columbia.

To the Honorable Senate and House of Representatives of the United States of America in Congress assembled, the petition of the undersigned citizens of Boston in Massachusetts and its vicinity respectfully represents—

That your petitioners are deeply impressed with the evils arising from the existence of slavery in the District of Columbia. While our Declaration of Independence boldly proclaims as self-evident truths, 'that all men are created equal, that they are endowed by their Creator with certain inalienable rights, that among these are life, liberty, and the pursuit of happiness,'—at the very seat of government human beings are born, almost daily, whom the laws pronounce to be from their birth, not *equal* to other men, and who are, for life, deprived of *liberty* and the free *pursuit of happiness*. The inconsistency of the conduct of our nation with its political creed, has brought down upon it the just and severe reprehension of foreign nations.

In addition to the other evils flowing from slavery, both moral and political, which it is needless to specify, circumstances have rendered this District a common resort for traders in human flesh, who bring into it their captives in chains, and lodge them in places of confinement, previously to their being carried to the markets of the south and west.

From the small number of slaves in the District of Columbia, and the moderate proportion which they bear to the free population there, the difficulties, which in most of the slaveholding states oppose the restoration of this degraded class of men to their natural rights, do not exist.

Your petitioners therefore pray that Congress will, without delay, take such measures for the immediate or gradual abolition of Slavery in the District of Columbia, and for preventing the bringing of slaves into that District for purposes of traffic, in such mode, as may be thought advisable; and that suitable provision be made for the education of all free blacks and colored children in the District, thus to preserve them from continuing, even as free men, an unenlightened and degraded caste.

If any individual should be unmoved, [illegible] by the petition or the introductory remarks, the following article will startle his apathy, unless he be morally dead. Read it—read it! The language of the editor [illegible] [illegible] considering the quarter whence it emanates. After all, we are not the only fanatics in the land!

[From the [illegible]]

THE SLAVE TRADE IN THE CAPITAL.

[illegible]
All bonds of nature in that moment end,
And each endures, while yet he draws his [illegible],
A stroke as fatal as the scythe of death;
They lose in tears, the far receding shore,
But not the thought that they must meet no more.

It is well, perhaps, the American people should know, that while we reiterate our boasts of liberty in the ears of the nations, and send back across the Atlantic our shouts of joy at the triumph of liberty in France, we ourselves are busily engaged in the work of oppression. Yes, let it be known to the citizens of America, that at the very time when the procession which contained the President of the United States and his Cabinet was marching in triumph to the Capitol, to celebrate the victory of the French people over their oppressors, another kind of procession was marching another way, and that consisted of colored human beings, handcuffed in pairs, and driven along by what had the appearance of a man on a horse! A similar scene was repeated on Saturday last; a drove consisting of males and females chained in couples, starting from Roby's tavern on foot, for Alexandria, where, with others, they are to embark on board a slave-ship in waiting to convey them to the South. While we are writing, a colored man enters our room, and begs us to inform him if we can point out any person who will redeem his friend now immured in Alexandria jail, in a state of distress amounting almost to distraction.* He has been a faithful servant of a revolutionary officer who recently died—has been sold at auction—parted from affectionate parents—and from decent and mourning friends. Our own servant, with others, of whom we can speak in commendatory terms, went down to Alexandria to bid him farewell, but they were refused admission to his cell, as was said, 'the sight of his friends made him feel so.' He bears the reputation of a pious man. It is but a few weeks since we saw a ship with her cargo of slaves in the port of Norfolk, Va.; on passing up the river, saw another ship off Alexandria, swarming with the victims of human cupidity. Such are the scenes enacting in the heart of the American nation. Oh patriotism! where is thy indignation? Oh philanthropy! where is thy grief? OH SHAME, WHERE IS THY BLUSH? Well may the generous and noble minded O'Connell say of the American citizen, '*I tell him he is a hypocrite. Look at the stain in your star-spangled standard that was never struck down in battle. I turn from the Declaration of American Independence, and I tell him that he has declared to God and man a lie, and before God and man I arraign him as a hypocrite.*' Yes, thou soul of fire, glorious O'Connell, if thou could but witness the spectacles in Washington that make the genius of liberty droop her head in shame, and weep her tears away in deep silence and undissembled sorrow, you would lift your voice even to tones of thunder, but you would make yourself heard. Where is the O'Connell of this republic that will plead for the EMANCIPATION OF THE DISTRICT OF COLUMBIA? These shocking scenes must cease from amongst us, or we must cease to call ourselves free; ay, and we must cease to expect the mercy of God—we must prepare for the coming judgment of Him who, as our charter acknowledges, made all men '*free and equal!*'

* At the [illegible] was sold, another [illegible] bought—was knocked off. The tears and agonies of his wife made such no impression on the mind of a generous speculator that he bought him back.

When a premium of Fifty Dollars is offered for the best theatrical poem, our newspapers advertise the fact with great unanimity. The following is incomparably more important.

A Premium of Fifty Dollars, the Donation of a benevolent individual in the State of Maine, and now deposited with the Treasurer of the Pennsylvania Society for promoting the Abolition of Slavery, &c. is offered to the author of the best Treatise on the following subject: 'The Duties of Ministers and Churches of all denominations to avoid the stain of Slavery, and to make the holding of Slaves a barrier to communion and church membership.'

The composition to be directed (post paid) to either of the subscribers—the name of the author in a separate sealed paper, which will be destroyed if his work shall be rejected.

Six months from this date are allowed for the purpose of receiving the Essays.

The publication and circulation of the preferred Tract will be regulated by the Pennsylvania Society above mentioned.

W. RAWLE,
J. PRESTON, } *Committee.*
THOMAS SHIPLEY,
Philadelphia, Oct. 11.

In his newspaper, The Liberator, *Garrison spoke out against the injustices of slavery.*

them was Gabriel Prosser, a slave in Virginia. In 1800, Prosser, along with his brothers Martin and Solomon, made plans to attack Richmond, the capital of Virginia. They intended to capture a large supply of weapons and take the governor, James Monroe, hostage. However, Prosser's plans were betrayed by two slaves, and he was captured and hanged.

Toussaint L'Ouverture helped free the slaves of Hispaniola and established an independent government.

Although the South dealt harshly with slaves who led revolts, this did not stop others from planning to do the same thing. Denmark Vesey had been owned by a slave trader who took him to Haiti, where he learned about L'Ouverture's slave uprising. In 1800, Vesey bought his freedom and set up a carpentry shop in Charleston. Later, he became a member of the African Methodist Episcopal Church, which attracted many black members. This worried white planters, who feared that the church could eventually spark a revolution. In 1821, the authorities closed the church Vesey attended. Although he was a free man with a successful business, Vesey realized that the rights of every black person were in jeopardy as long as white planters controlled the government. He began planning a slave rebellion. Vesey was careful not to reveal his entire plan to any of his followers for fear that he might be betrayed. Nevertheless, Charleston officials eventually discovered the plot. At first, they were not sure who was leading the rebellion. But their investigations gradually brought them to Vesey. He was arrested and hanged, along with several of his co-conspirators.

Ten years after Vesey's hanging, a slave named Nat Turner led a revolt in Virginia that sent shock waves through the South. Turner was a respected preacher who claimed to have visions that whites and blacks would kill each other. One of these visions sparked his rebellion, which began on August 22, 1831. With a few followers, Turner attacked the homes of slave owners, killing their families and stealing their weapons. But Turner proved no match for the local militia, which killed some of his men in a bloody skirmish. Turner managed to escape and hide for weeks in the Dismal Swamp in North Carolina. Meanwhile, rumors swept the area that he was leading an enormous rebellion that threatened the lives of white citizens. Eventually, he was captured. Turner was rapidly brought before a judge, where he pleaded guilty and was hanged.

Many Southerners blamed the abolitionists, especially William Lloyd Garrison, for encouraging Nat Turner's rebellion. Garrison was personally opposed to violence but thought it might be necessary to overthrow slavery. In his newspaper, *The Liberator*, Garrison called Turner's revolt the first step on the road to freedom. "The first step of the earthquake, which is ultimately to shake down the fabric of oppression, leaving not one stone upon the other, has been made," Garrison wrote. "The first drops of blood, which are but the prelude to a deluge from the gathering clouds, have fallen."[2] The fears generated by Turner's rebellion gradually subsided, although slave codes were made harsher to prevent more revolts.

The *Amistad* incident occurred only eight years later. It looked to Southerners like another slave rebellion. Southern newspapers claimed that Cinqué and the other Africans were Spanish property, because they were slaves sold in Cuba. Southerners opposed any effort by the abolitionists to defend the Africans.

They believed that the Africans should be returned to Cuba to stand trial for murder and rebellion.

Reactions in the North

As opposition in the South mounted, Dwight Janes continued his efforts to make sure that the Africans of the *Amistad* received a fair hearing. He wrote to Roger S. Baldwin, a prominent New Haven lawyer, hoping he would defend Cinqué and his followers. Janes also sent a letter to Joshua Leavitt of New York, an editor of *The Emancipator*, published by the Anti-Slavery Society. Janes asked Leavitt to find an interpreter for Cinqué so he could tell his side of the story. Early in September, Leavitt, along with Lewis Tappan and Simeon Jocelyn, a Congregational minister in New Haven, were appointed members of the *Amistad* Committee, made up of men from the area. It was charged with raising a legal defense fund for the Africans and ensuring that they were well cared for during the time they spent in the New Haven jail.

In New Haven, the adult Africans had been confined in three rooms, while the four children had a room to themselves. Cinqué was jailed by himself because he was considered more violent than the rest of the captives. Doctors who examined the prisoners found that they were suffering from malnutrition. Because they were far from home and fearful of the future, many of them were too depressed to eat. Indeed, one had already died and others were sick.

Source Document

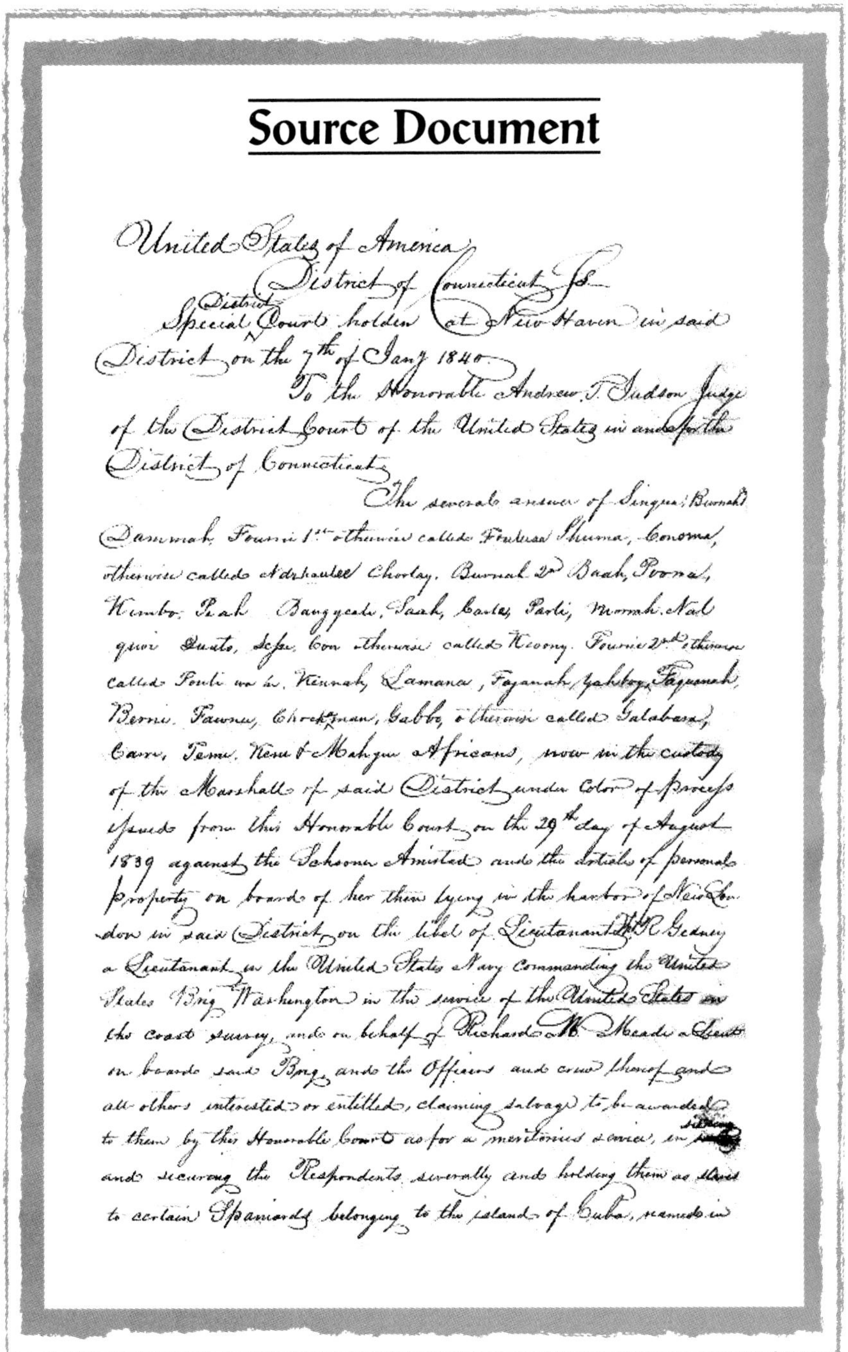

United States of America
District of Connecticut ss.
Special District Court holden at New Haven in said
District on the 7th of Jany 1840
To the Honorable Andrew T. Judson Judge
of the District Court of the United States in and for the
District of Connecticut
The several answer of Singua; Burnah 1st
Dammah, Founi 1st otherwise called Fuliwa Shuma, Conoma,
otherwise called Ndzhaulee Cherlay, Burnah 2d Baah, Poonah,
Kimbo, Peah, Bangyeah, Saah, Carle, Parli, Moorah, Nal
quoi Quato, Sese, Con otherwise called Kooony, Fouine 2d otherwise
called Pouli wa hi, Kinnah, Lamana, Fajanah, Yahboy, Faginah,
Berri, Fawne, Chockzman, Gabbo, otherwise called Galabara,
Carri, Teme, Kene & Mahgee Africans, now in the custody
of the Marshall of said District under Color of Process
issued from this Honorable Court on the 29th day of August
1839 against the Schooner Amistad and the Articles of personal
property on board of her then lying in the harbor of New London in said District on the libel of Lieutenant T. R. Gedney
a Lieutenant in the United States Navy commanding the United
States Brig Washington in the service of the United States in
the coast survey, and in behalf of Richard W. Meade a Lieut
on board said Brig and the Officers and crew thereof and
all others interested or entitled, claiming salvage to be awarded
to them by this Honorable Court as for a meritorious service, in seizing
and securing the Respondents severally and holding them as slaves
to certain Spaniards belonging to the island of Cuba, named in

Several prominent abolitionists wrote this statement about their decision to help the Africans.

Meanwhile, the *Amistad* Committee continued its efforts to free the Africans. They took out advertisements in newspapers, asking for contributions to the defense fund. Lewis Tappan wrote letters that were printed in the papers, trying to win sympathy for the prisoners. He also located an African in New York

Joseph Cinqué's leadership during the revolt made him the central figure in the Amistad *trials. "Cinqué," however, was not his real name. It had been changed from "Singbe-pieh" by the Spanish slave traders to make him appear to be a resident of Cuba.*

named John Ferry who might be able to communicate with the captives. Ferry talked to the Africans and seemed to understand some of their language. He believed that the children had been taken from Africa and sold as slaves. Meanwhile, newspaper accounts focused on Cinqué, who was rapidly becoming a celebrity. In local stores, people could buy wax figures and portraits of Cinqué and the other Africans. Five thousand people paid to see the prisoners in the New Haven jail. A play titled *The Pirate Slaver "Amistad"* opened in New York to large audiences.[3]

Reactions to the *Amistad* captives in the North were mixed. While some newspapers agreed with the abolitionists that the Africans should be freed, others disagreed. Some believed that the blacks were better off in a state of slavery, that they were no better than apes and monkeys, and that the natural state of affairs between whites and blacks should be as master and slave. Northern journalists also criticized abolitionists like the Tappans for being publicity seekers.[4] As the *New York Morning Herald* put it: "The Abolitionists are determined to baffle those desirous of justice. . . . All the whining . . . is . . . without the color of truth to support it."[5]

The newspapers reflected the attitudes of many Northerners toward slavery. They generally felt that this matter should be left to the South to handle. Northern industrialists who ran cotton mills recognized that they had a stake in slavery because several million slaves were necessary to pick cotton. Wage earners in the North also feared that a large population of free blacks might compete with them for jobs. A Frenchman named Alexis de Tocqueville, who traveled extensively in America during the 1830s, wrote about Northern racism in his book *Democracy in America*:

> Whoever has inhabited the United States must have perceived that in those parts of the Union in which the Negroes are no longer slaves they have in no wise drawn nearer to the whites. . . . On the contrary, the prejudice of race appears to be stronger in the states that have abolished slavery than in those where it still exists. . . .[6]

Indeed, racism existed in many parts of the North. Free blacks had lost the right to vote in New York, Connecticut, New Jersey, and Pennsylvania. In Philadelphia, they were forced to attend segregated schools. In Canterbury, Connecticut, Prudence Crandall had tried to admit black children to her private school. White parents were so angry that they withdrew their children. When Crandall tried to start a school for blacks, townspeople lobbied the state legislature, which passed a law forbidding such a school to open. Crandall went to jail when she tried to defy the law. Later, when she wanted to reopen her school, the townspeople tried to burn down the building.

Much of the racism in the North was focused on the abolitionists. In 1834, for example, a mob stormed a meeting of the American Anti-Slavery Society and looted Lewis Tappan's home. A year later, in Boston, another mob left William Lloyd Garrison battered and bruised. But the strength of the abolitionists continued to increase during the 1830s as local antislavery societies spread across the Northern states. Now the abolitionists hoped that the *Amistad* case would focus national attention, once and for all, on the evil institution of slavery.

Van Buren Hesitates

For its efforts to be successful, the *Amistad* Committee believed it was in a desperate race against time. The committee feared that President Martin Van Buren might act quickly to dispose of the case without a public trial. A Democrat, Van Buren held together a fragile coalition of Northerners and Southerners who had elected him in 1836. He planned to run for re-election in 1840 and he needed the support of the Southern slaveholders to ensure a victory. If the *Amistad* prisoners were freed as a result of a trial, it would definitely anger the South and cause him to lose the upcoming election.

Van Buren hoped he could solve this problem by simply honoring the treaty obligations that existed between Spain and the United States. According to Pinckney's Treaty of 1795, a Spanish ship and its cargo that had been forced into an American port by pirates should be returned to the control of Spain. On September 6, 1839, Spanish minister Angel Calderón de la Barca called on Van Buren to return the *Amistad* to Cuba under the terms of the treaty. Cinqué, according to the minister, had led a mutiny on a Spanish ship in Spanish waters. The United States, he said, had no authority over this matter. The minister wanted the Africans to stand trial in Cuba for mutiny and murder. Finally, the Spanish believed that the United States should take the same position regarding these prisoners as it did with regard to its own slaves—namely, murder is not sanctioned in the name of achieving freedom. In other words, the *Amistad* Africans had no right to kill the crew members on the ship just to win their freedom.

President Van Buren wanted to go along with the Spanish minister's request. The United States district attorney in Connecticut, William S. Holabird, was immediately contacted by the Van Buren administration. Holabird would be involved in the case when it came up before the grand jury. He was warned by Secretary of State John Forsythe not to let the situation get "beyond the control of the Federal Executive."[7] Forsythe had already promised the Spanish minister that he would keep things under control. Clearly, the Van Buren administration was prepared to prevent the case from going too far. The administration had directed Holabird to get the case dismissed as soon as it went to court in Connecticut.

However, the president would soon discover that the *Amistad* incident was already taking on a life of its own. And there was little that he or his administration could do to stop it.

Chapter 5

The Trials Begin

In September 1839, as the circuit court convened in Hartford, Connecticut, to hear the *Amistad* case, author William Cullen Bryant published a poem about Cinqué in the pages of *The Emancipator*:

Chained in a foreign land he stood,
A man of giant frame,
Amid the gathering multitude
That shrunk to hear his name—
All stern of look and strong of limb,
His dark eye on the ground—
And silently they gazed on him
As on a lion *bound.*

Vainly, but well, that chief had fought—
He was a captive now;
Yet pride, that fortune humbles not,
Was written on his brow.
The scars his dark broad bosom wore
Showed warrior true and brave;
A prince among his tribe before,
He could not be a slave.[1]

During the weeks leading up to the hearing, the abolitionists had tried to create the nineteenth-century equivalent of a media event by building as much support as possible for Cinqué and his fellow Africans. So far, this effort had been highly successful. The hotels in Hartford were crowded with people from as far away as Boston. They had come to see the prisoners as they were brought up from the New Haven jail. On the day the trial began, the courtroom was packed with onlookers and members of the press. Throughout the rest of the country, the abolitionists had also succeeded in focusing attention on the *Amistad* courtroom. From Cincinnati, Ohio, abolitionist James G. Birney wrote to Lewis Tappan, "The public sympathy here is decidedly in favor of the Africans at Hartford."[2] The *New London Gazette and General Advertiser* said that the slaves had been "feloniously [illegally] kidnapped and sold," adding, "was there not much . . . to justify them in acting as they did to regain that liberty and those rights of which they had been so wickedly deprived?"[3] Opinion in the South, however, was against the captives. A newspaper in Charleston referred to the *Amistad* Africans as a "piratical crew . . . their hands still reeking with the blood of murdered men. . . ."[4]

The Hearing Opens

Presiding over the United States circuit court, Judge Smith Thompson listened as the lawyers for each side presented their arguments. The case before him involved charges of murder, mutiny, and piracy against

James G. Birney, a friend of Lewis Tappan's, ran as a presidential candidate for the Liberty party, an abolitionist group.

Cinqué and the other prisoners. In addition, there were various claims against the *Amistad* and its cargo. Lieutenant Gedney of the U.S.S. *Washington* was claiming that he and his men were entitled to some reward, called salvage, for capturing the *Amistad* and the Africans on board. Captain Henry Green was also represented by a lawyer in court, who claimed that Green had detained Cinqué long enough for Gedney's men to capture him. In addition, Ruiz and Montes were represented by counsel, who demanded that the two Spaniards were entitled to have their slaves returned. Finally, United States Attorney William S. Holabird presented a claim from the Spanish government demanding that the *Amistad* and its captives be returned to Spain under the terms of Pinckney's Treaty.

On Thursday afternoon, September 19, attorney Roger Baldwin, representing the Africans, asked for a writ of habeas corpus for the three girls who had been aboard the *Amistad*. John Barber, who attended the trial, wrote that the "three African girls were brought into Court weeping, and evidently much terrified at the separation from their companions:—the eldest being about eleven years old."[5] Under a writ of habeas corpus, the girls were entitled to be freed if Baldwin could show that they were being held unlawfully because they had committed no crime. It was a bold strategy by the defense. Baldwin hoped to win sympathy from the judge by focusing the hearing on the defenseless little girls. He also gambled that, if the girls were released under the writ of habeas corpus, it might mean that the judge would consider making the same decision for the other captives. This would be an admission that they were not slaves, but free human beings. As free human beings, they had had every right to rebel against Ruiz and Montes, who held them illegally. Therefore, they should be released from jail immediately.

Holabird, representing the government, strongly disagreed. He argued that the Africans were property that should be returned to the Spanish government. Nevertheless, he did state that, if the blacks had illegally been brought from Africa in violation of the international agreements regarding the slave trade, then they should be returned to their homeland. On Friday, Theodore Sedgwick—a member of the *Amistad* defense team—continued to present arguments in favor of the writ of habeas corpus. He produced evidence from interpreter John Ferry that the Africans had not been residents of Cuba but had been kidnapped from their homelands. However, Ralph Ingersoll, representing Ruiz and Montes, argued that there was no convincing evidence to prove that the Africans were not the legal property of his clients.

Nevertheless, the defense seemed to be gradually winning its case. This may have explained why United States Attorney Holabird finally stood up to make an unexpected announcement. "I stand here to contend that these blacks are free men—that they have been brought within the jurisdiction of the United States," he said, "and if found to be, as I suppose, native Africans, they may be sent to their native land."[6]

The Judge's Decision

After presenting their arguments, the lawyers for each side could now only sit and wait for Judge Thompson to deliver his verdict. As the judge began to speak, everyone in the courtroom listened closely. Thompson explained that the Africans could not stand trial in the United States for mutiny and murder, because their actions had taken place on board a Spanish ship in Spanish waters. Therefore, the United States courts had no jurisdiction over this matter. He denied the writ of habeas corpus. Instead, he said that the United States district court must decide whether the Africans were slaves and should be returned to Ruiz and Montes. He also said that the district court had to rule on the claims by Gedney and Green.

Thus, the abolitionists had rescued Cinqué and his companions from a murder charge. But they could still be returned to Cuba as slaves. There, they would probably stand trial and face execution.

Following the verdict, Judge Andrew Judson called the district court to order in Hartford, where the remaining issues would be heard. However, the case was postponed until November 19, to await more evidence that was important to the case. Judson was willing to grant bail for the Africans in the amount of their value as Cuban slaves. But the abolitionists would not admit that they were slaves, so Cinqué and his companions were returned to jail. Conditions improved for them, however. They were allowed to exercise outside, and the children were moved to a nearby private home.

The Case Takes a New Turn

While the district court was not in session, the *Amistad* case continued to be played out in the press. Ruiz and Montes told their story, claiming that they had not subjected the Africans to harsh treatment aboard ship. Meanwhile, the abolitionists searched for another interpreter to replace John Ferry. He had very little understanding of the language spoken by Cinqué and many of his companions. Eventually, an interpreter was found by Professor Josiah Gibbs of Yale University. James Covey was a linguist who tried to talk with Cinqué and believed he was speaking in Mende. Covey had been kidnapped from Mende country and forced aboard a slave ship headed for the Americas. Fortunately, the ship was stopped by a British patrol boat. Covey was freed, and eventually, he joined the British Navy. He was currently serving on a ship that was anchored in New York Harbor.

Covey found it easy to communicate with Cinqué, who described a long saga beginning with his capture in the African bush, his journey to the stifling barracoon of Pedro Blanco, and the terrible voyage across the Atlantic on the slave ship *Tecora*.

Cinqué then explained how he was smuggled into Cuba, where the Africans were eventually purchased by Ruiz and Montes. Finally, he described the revolt aboard the *Amistad*. Cinqué's story, along with those of other captives, was told through Covey to members of the press who had come to the New Haven jail.

Meanwhile, Lewis Tappan had decided on a bold move to throw Ruiz and Montes off balance. He persuaded Cinqué and several of the other Africans to file lawsuits charging the two Spaniards with assault, kidnapping, and wrongful imprisonment. Ruiz and Montes were arrested in New York and put into jail. Although Montes posted bail and left the country, Ruiz remained in confinement. However, Tappan's strategy backfired. The Spanish government was angry that two of its citizens were being jailed. Many Americans also believed the abolitionists had gone too far. As the New York *Courier & Enquirer* put it, they were "making sport of the law and perverting the power of the courts of justice to . . . fanatical ends."[7]

Preparing for the Trial in District Court

In November, Judge Judson continued the trial in district court. Roger Baldwin raised the issue of whether Connecticut had jurisdiction over the *Amistad* case, because Lieutenant Gedney had captured the ship and the Africans in New York. The abolitionists were trying to move the case to New York. They believed that there was strong racial prejudice in Connecticut, as shown by the Prudence Crandall case in 1831. In fact,

Abolitionist Lewis Tappan was one of the strongest defenders of the Amistad *captives.*

Andrew Judson was the man who had led the fight to close down Crandall's school. Thus, the abolitionists feared he might not give their case a fair hearing.

Judson listened to Baldwin's argument as well as the salvage claims of Lieutenant Gedney and Henry Green. However, he did not make any final decisions. Instead, he postponed the trial until January in New Haven. Meanwhile, he heard testimony from Dr. Richard Madden, which was directly relevant to the case. Madden had lived in Cuba, serving on a commission that dealt with slave ships captured by British warships. These slavers had tried to bring their cargoes onto the island illegally. He was also responsible for the protection of the blacks who had been freed because they were brought to Cuba. Madden spoke to the captives in New Haven. He became convinced that they were *bozales*—slaves who had been brought to Cuba illegally—not *ladinos*—residents of Cuba before the slave trade had become illegal. Many of the Africans were simply too young to have been longtime residents of the island. They also spoke no Spanish. Madden presented this testimony to Judge Judson.

The Hearing in District Court

As the day of the district court hearing in New Haven came closer, the stakes in the case grew even bigger. The Spanish government, referring to the Africans as "assassins," demanded that they be returned to Cuba immediately.[8] The case had already gone on far too long for the administration of President Martin Van

Buren. It was dividing opinions in the North and South, which might cost Van Buren his re-election. Attorney General Felix Grundy prepared a document stating that the Africans on the *Amistad* were slaves who belonged to Ruiz and Montes. The *Amistad*, Grundy said, was not involved in the illegal slave trade when the revolt occurred. The ship and its cargo should, therefore, be returned to Spanish control under the terms of Pinckney's Treaty.

Van Buren expected that the district court would agree with the attorney general and order the blacks to be sent back to Cuba. The administration told the Spanish that an American ship, the schooner U.S.S. *Grampus*, would be standing by in New Haven harbor to take the Africans immediately back to Havana. United States Attorney Holabird was also secretly instructed to transport the Africans to the *Grampus* before their lawyers had time to present an appeal. Thus, the administration was prepared to sidestep the legal system to achieve its goals and not let attorneys for the Africans appeal a decision that would send them back to Cuba as slaves.

The *Grampus*, under the command of Lieutenant John Paine, was anchored in New Haven harbor as the hearing resumed in Judge Judson's court. This time, Dwight Janes was called to the witness stand. He testified that Ruiz had admitted that the blacks had come from Africa. Testimony from James Covey confirmed that the Africans had been illegally transported to Cuba as slaves.

Attorney General Felix Grundy argued that the Amistad *captives should be returned to Spain under Pinckney's Treaty.*

By far the most electrifying moment of the hearing occurred when the tall, muscular Cinqué strode slowly forward. Taking the oath, he gave his testimony. Cinqué told his story through the interpreter, James Covey. There had been rumors that Cinqué himself had been a slave trader, selling a man into slavery to pay off his debt. But he strongly denied this. John Barber, an eyewitness to the court proceedings, explained that Cinqué also

> described by actions, (which spoke louder than words,) the manner in which . . . [Ruiz] examined the Africans to ascertain if they were healthy and sound [examining their genital area]. He also put himself in the position in which they were forced to remain, when packed away on board the slaver.[9]

Afterward, two other Africans, Grabeau and Fuliwa, testified to the same facts. The prosecution tried to show that Cinqué had lied about being a slave trader. They also tried to prove that Dr. Madden's testimony was inaccurate. Holabird claimed that the blacks did not speak Spanish because they had continued to communicate in their native language long after arriving in Cuba. In addition, he said the *Amistad* had been authorized by the Cuban authorities to transport slaves from one port to another on the island. Meanwhile, Gedney's lawyer also presented his claim for a reward for capturing the ship and the Africans on board.

On January 13, 1840, Judge Judson finally handed down his decision. He ruled that the district court was authorized to hear the case because Gedney had captured the *Amistad* on the high seas, not in New York waters. Therefore, the case could come to trial in the state where he had landed the ship, Connecticut. Gedney was also entitled to salvage for his efforts—one third of the value of the vessel and its cargo. The *Amistad* and its cargo should then be returned to the Spanish government.

Finally, Judson answered the larger question: Were the Africans part of the ship's cargo? Were they

Grabeau was one of the Africans aboard the Amistad *who helped Cinqué carry out his rebellion.*

Judge Judson decided in district court that the captives of Amistad *were free people who had the right to return to Africa. The Africans celebrated after hearing the news.*

property or were they free human beings? This was the decision that everyone in the courtroom had been waiting to hear. Judson ruled that the Africans had been brought into Cuba illegally. They were not slaves, but free men. Therefore, they had a right to rebel in order to regain their liberty. They could not be sent back to Cuba to stand trial for murder. They "shall not sigh for Africa in vain," he said. "Bloody as may be their hands, they shall yet embrace their kindred."[10] He ordered that they be handed over to President Van Buren and placed on an American ship that would take them back to west Africa.

Cinqué and his companions were finally going home.

Chapter 6

The *Amistad* and the Supreme Court

About the time of the trial in district court, Cinqué, who was just learning the basic elements of English, wrote a short letter to abolitionist Lewis Tappan: "I will write you a few lines because I loves you very much," he began. "Cinque want you to go and See him. . . . make this Menda men free to go to African. . . . O please to let us go to the Africa. . . ."[1]

Judge Judson's decision had apparently granted Cinqué his wish. He said they were "free" to go to Africa. But it was not quite the freedom Tappan and the other abolitionists had hoped for. Judson said he was carrying out a law passed by Congress more than twenty years earlier. It stated that it was unlawful to bring a black person from another country into the United States as a slave. The law also gave the president the authority to return that person home. But men who were truly free, Tappan knew, were not handed over to anyone—not even the president—to be taken anywhere. They were free to go wherever they wanted. Cinqué and his companions were not to be given the same rights as free whites in America—even though Judson had ruled that the blacks were free. The abolitionists had hoped that Cinqué and the other Africans would achieve equal footing with white Americans. This would be a first step to achieving equality for all blacks. However, Judson's decision had not given the *Amistad* captives this equality.

If this were not disappointing enough, at least as far as Tappan and the abolitionists were concerned, the administration of President Martin Van Buren then decided to challenge Judson's decision. United States District Attorney William S. Holabird was instructed to appeal the judge's ruling. Cinqué and the other Africans were not to be freed, after all.

Of course, Cinqué was extremely disappointed. What was this system of American justice that set a man free in one breath, only to keep him behind bars in the next? Holabird's appeal was heard at the next meeting of the circuit court, in April 1840, with Judge Judson and Judge Smith Thompson presiding. As everyone expected, they simply upheld the rulings made by their earlier courts.

This set up a final appeal by the government to the United States Supreme Court, the highest court in America. The Supreme Court justices agreed to hear the case in early 1841. It would prove to be a titanic struggle—with the freedom of Cinqué and the other *Amistad* captives hanging in the balance.

Adams Enters the Case

Meanwhile, the African captives were moved out of New Haven to confinement in Westville, a few miles away. Students from Yale University visited regularly, instructing the Africans in Christianity, teaching them prayers, and helping them learn to read and write. Kali, a ten-year-old African boy who had been aboard the *Amistad*, seemed to learn English more rapidly than his companions. In 1841, he wrote a lengthy letter to former President John Quincy Adams, a strong opponent of slavery, who had been closely following the *Amistad* case:

> I want to write a letter to you because you love Mendi people and you talk to the grand court. We want to tell you one thing—Jose Ruiz say we born in Havana, he tell lie. . . . We all born in Mendi—we no understand the Spanish language. . . . We talk American language little, not very good; we write every day: we write plenty letters; we read most all time; we read all Matthew and Mark, and Luke, and John [books of the New Testament of the Bible], and plenty of little books. We love books very much. We want you to ask the court what we have done wrong. What for Americans keep us in prison.[2]

Lewis Tappan realized that the Africans' last chance to achieve freedom was the nine justices who sat on the United States Supreme Court. Five of them, including Chief Justice Roger B. Taney of Maryland, were Southerners who might vote to send the Africans

Kali was one of the Africans in the Amistad *trial.*

back to Cuba. Therefore, he reasoned, he needed someone with a national reputation and experience arguing cases in front of the nation's highest court to speak for the Africans. At first, Tappan approached Daniel Webster, a distinguished lawyer and United States senator. But he declined. Webster was busy and said he did not want to present a case before the Supreme Court. Tappan then decided to ask John Quincy Adams to represent the *Amistad* captives.

Adams was one of America's most experienced statesmen. When he was eleven years old, he had traveled to Europe as secretary to his father, John Adams, who had been sent to France to seek aid for the American Revolution. Later, John Quincy Adams would lead his own diplomatic missions as ambassador to Prussia and Russia. He also served as secretary of state during the administration of President James Monroe, becoming chief architect of the famous Monroe Doctrine. Elected president in 1824, Adams served only one term in the White House. He retired to Massachusetts, where he was elected a congressman in 1830.

As biographer Paul Nagel pointed out, Adams was never an abolitionist, but he was strongly opposed to slavery. In 1836, the House of Representatives had passed the gag rule, which prevented petitions opposed to slavery from being read on the House floor. Adams, who strongly supported free speech, did everything possible to overturn that rule and undermine the power of the slaveholders. "His adopted cause transformed him into a debater so impassioned, so mischievous, so stubborn, and so radical," Nagel wrote, "that his foes and even some friends wondered at times if he had lost his sanity."[3]

Adams was seventy-three years old when Tappan approached him. He had not argued a case before the Supreme Court in many years. No one knew his own shortcomings better than Adams, and at first, he declined the offer to handle the case. But Tappan insisted that he reconsider, and Adams finally agreed. He would join Roger Baldwin for the defense.

Meanwhile, Adams had successfully pushed a bill through Congress requiring the Van Buren administration to make public all correspondence relating to the *Amistad* case. As this information came out, Northern newspapers began printing articles claiming that Van Buren and Secretary of State John Forsyth seemed to have been supporting the position of the slave traders, Ruiz and Montes, as well as the government of Spain. When Ruiz and Montes were jailed, for example, Forsyth had told one of the government's legal officers to give them advice and aid

John Quincy Adams was in his seventies when he took on the Amistad *case, but his outstanding legal mind was as sharp as ever.*

that would help them win their freedom. In addition, the ship *Grampus* had been standing by during the district court trial to take the Africans back to Cuba, without waiting for their lawyers to file an appeal.

Adams would use this apparently improper interference by the Van Buren administration as his main line of argument during the Supreme Court trial. In addition, he met with Baldwin in New Haven and visited with Cinqué and his fellow Africans in jail. But even as he tried to prepare a strong case, Adams was forced to battle his own physical infirmities. "An inflammation in my left eye threatens me with complete disability to perform my final duty before the Supreme Court in the case of the *Amistad* captives," he wrote in his diary, "while the daily and hourly increasing weight of the pressure of preparation aggravates that disability."[4]

Adams was under no illusion as to the enormous task confronting him, although he may have been prone to overstate the role that he had been asked to play. He said:

> No one else will undertake it; no one but a spirit unconquerable by man, woman or fiend can undertake it but with the heart of martyrdom [dying for a cause]. The world, the flesh, and all the devils in hell are arrayed against any man who now in this North American Union shall dare to join the standard of Almighty God to put down the African slave-trade. . . .[5]

The Case Reaches the Supreme Court

The case opened on February 22, 1841. United States Attorney General Henry D. Gilpin presented the government's arguments as he paced back and forth before the justices. He argued that documents on the *Amistad* showed that the Africans were slaves owned by Ruiz and Montes, and should be returned to their owners under the terms of Pinckney's Treaty. Gilpin asked the justices to disregard testimony received from witnesses such as Dr. Madden.

Roger Baldwin then began his presentation. He stated that Cinqué and the others were not slaves, but free men unlawfully held by Ruiz and Montes. Once Baldwin was done, John Quincy Adams then rose to speak:

> The charge I make against the present Executive administration is that in all their proceedings relating to these unfortunate men, instead of that *Justice*, which they were bound not less than this honorable Court itself to observe, they have substituted *Sympathy!*—sympathy with one of the parties in this conflict of justice, and *Antipathy* [opposition] to the other. Sympathy with the white, antipathy to the black. . . .[6]

Adams then tried to demonstrate that, throughout the course of the *Amistad* case, the Van Buren administration had consistently given in to the demands of the Spanish government that the ship and the Africans be returned to their control. He cited a letter from Secretary of State John Forsyth to District Attorney Holabird, shortly after the ship was captured by Lieutenant Gedney. The letter stated that no action by the courts should place "the vessel, cargo, or slaves beyond the control of the Federal Executive."[8] Adams then cited evidence showing that President Martin Van Buren's administration intended to help Ruiz and Montes when they were in jail. The administration had also planned to smuggle the Africans onto the waiting ship *Grampus*—if the decision were made to return them to Cuba—without waiting to allow their lawyers the opportunity to make an appeal. The Spanish wanted public vengeance, Adams said. "What public vengeance? The vengeance of African slave-traders, despoiled of their prey and thirsting for blood! The vengeance of the barracoons! This 'public vengeance' is not satisfied."[8]

Adams completed his presentation after speaking to the Supreme Court justices for more than four hours. He was supposed to continue speaking the next day. However, one of the justices—Philip P. Barbour—died unexpectedly that evening, and the case was not resumed until March 1. When the Court reconvened, Adams made another lengthy speech. He was followed by Attorney General Gilpin, who stated

Source Document

MAY IT PLEASE YOUR HONORS—

. . . in a consideration of this case, I derive, in the distress I feel both for myself and my clients, consolation from two sources–first, that the rights of my clients to their lives and liberties have already been defended by my learned friend and colleague in so able and complete a manner as leaves me scarcely anything to say, and I feel that such full justice has been done to their interests, that any fault or imperfection of mine will merely be attributed to its true cause; and secondly, I derive consolation from the thought that this Court is a Court of JUSTICE. And in saying so very trivial a thing I should not on any other occasion, perhaps, be warranted in asking the Court to consider what justice is. Justice, as defined in the Institutes of Justinian, nearly 2000 years ago, and as it felt and understood by all who understand human relations and human rights, is—

"Constans et perpetua voluntas, jus suum cuique tribuendi."

"The constant and perpetual will to secure to every one HIS OWN right."

And in a Court of Justice, where there are two parties present, justice demands that the rights of each party should be allowed to himself, as well as that each party has a right, to be secured and protected by the Court.[9]

John Quincy Adams argued his case brilliantly before the United States Supreme Court.

that President Van Buren had not interfered with the case and re-emphasized that the Africans should not be freed.

A Final Decision

On March 9, the Court announced its decision. It was delivered by Justice Joseph Story, an opponent of slavery. The Africans were not slaves, Story said, and they should be freed. Furthermore, they had not been brought to America as slaves, but had been in control of the *Amistad* when it reached American waters. Therefore, they should not be handed over to the president. They should have the freedom to decide where they wanted to go. They were not pirates or robbers who had taken control of a ship. They had acted in self-defense to free themselves after being placed illegally in bondage.

When the decision had been handed down, the jailer and the United States marshal delivered the news to Cinqué and his companions in Westville. As one newspaper reported: "They were all

Justice Joseph Story delivered the Supreme Court decision that finally allowed the captives to go home.

Source Document

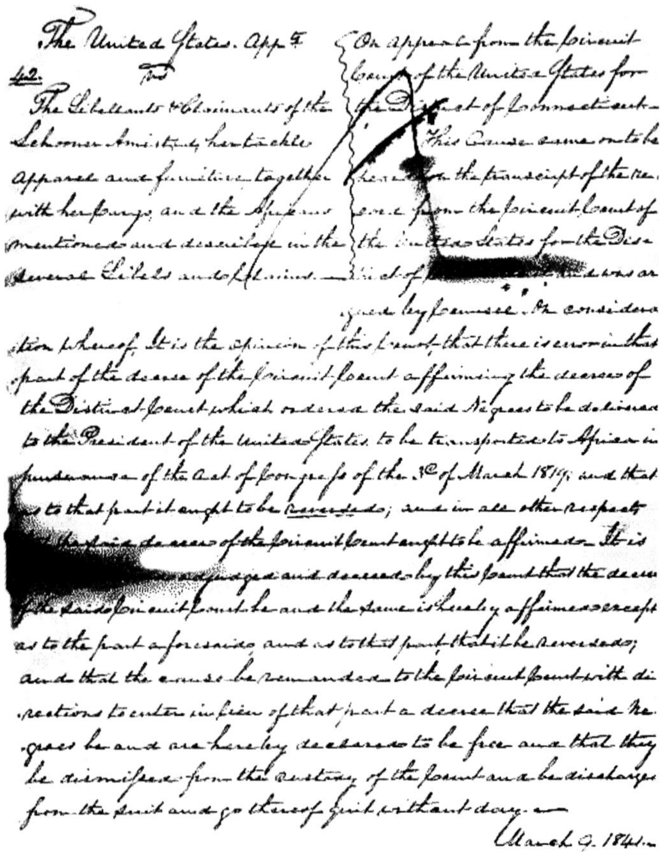

The United States. Appts.
42. vs
The Libellants & Claimants of the Schooner Amistad, her tackle, apparel and furniture, together with her cargo, and the Africans mentioned and described in the several Libels and Claims. —

On appeal from the Circuit Court of the United States for the District of Connecticut. This Cause came on to be heard on the transcript of the record from the Circuit Court of the United States for the District of [illegible] and was argued by counsel. On consideration whereof, It is the opinion of this Court, that there is error in that part of the decree of the Circuit Court affirming the decree of the District Court which ordered the said Negroes to be delivered to the President of the United States, to be transported to Africa in pursuance of the Act of Congress of the 3rd of March 1819; and that as to that part it ought to be reversed; and in all other respects that the said decree of the Circuit Court ought to be affirmed. It is [illegible] ordered and decreed by this Court that the decree of the said Circuit Court be and the same is hereby affirmed except as to the part aforesaid and as to that part that it be reversed; and that the cause be remanded to the Circuit Court with directions to enter in lieu of that part a decree that the said Negroes be and are hereby declared to be free and that they be dismissed from the custody of the Court and be discharged from the suit and go thereof quit without day. —

March 9. 1841. —

A page from the Supreme Court's decision in the Amistad *case.*

assembled in one room, and on a signal from Cinque were seated. . . . The Marshal then showed them a newspaper and said 'here it is in the paper—read it.' Cinque beckoned to little Kali to read it aloud. . . ."[10]

There would be no more appeals. America's highest court had made a final ruling. This time, the Africans were really free.

Later, Cinqué would write a letter to John Quincy Adams:

> Most Respected Sir,—the Mendi people give you thanks for all your kindness to them. They will never forget your defence of their rights before the great Court of Washington. They feel that they owe to you in a large measure, their delivery from the Spaniards, and from slavery or death. They will pray for you as long as you live, Mr. Adams. May God bless and reward you.[11]

Chapter 7

The *Amistad* in History

After Cinqué and the other captives were released from jail, they went to Farmington, Connecticut, to live on the farm of A. F. Williams. Farmington was one of the stations in the Underground Railroad, the network of people who helped runaway slaves escape to the North and Canada. There, the Africans continued with their religious education and their tutoring in English for six hours each day during the week.

Because they were no longer in the custody of the federal government, Cinqué and his companions had to pay for their own food and clothing. They also wanted to raise the funds necessary to return home to Africa. While they were in Farmington, one of the Africans, named Foone, drowned in a canal, possibly committing suicide because he was so depressed at having been away from his homeland for such a long time. The other Africans were eager to get back to Mende country as soon as possible.

In order to raise the funds the Africans needed, the *Amistad* Committee arranged for them to go on tour. Many Americans had followed the captives' story in the newspapers, and they were willing to pay to see Cinqué and the others in person. "Sixteen meetings were held," reported one newspaper. "The Mendeans read . . . spelt, answered questions . . . related their history in our tongue, sang native songs . . . and Cinque always made an address in his native language. . . . After he had concluded Kinna [one of the other Africans] interpreted what he said."[1]

The Africans also asked for assistance from the administration of the new president, John Tyler. "Now we want to go home, very much, very soon," Cinqué wrote to the president. "We want to see no more snow."[2] But Tyler was unwilling to help them unless a majority of legislators in Congress agreed to approve the expenditure. Congress turned it down. Nevertheless, enough funds were raised from the public tour, private donations, and money from a missionary society that wanted to establish a mission in Sierra Leone, Africa. On November 27, 1841, the thirty-five survivors of the original fifty-three Africans from the *Amistad* boarded the ship *Gentleman* to return to Africa. As they left from Boston, Cinqué, Kinna, and Kali wrote to John Quincy Adams: "We are about to go home to Africa. We go to Sierra Leone first, and then we reach Mendi very quick. When we get to Mendi we shall tell

Source Document

Dear Sir:

We have reached Sierra Leone and one little while after we go Mendi and we get land very safely. Oh dear friend, pray to God. God will hear your prayer. We will pray for you; and God is very great, very good and kind. We have been on great water. Not any danger fell upon us. Oh, no. We never forget glorious God for these great blessings. How joyful we shall be. I never forget you. May God be blessed. Our blessed saviour Jesus Christ have done wondrous works. Dear Mr. Tappan, how I feel for these wondrous things. I pray Jesus will hear you; if I never see you in this world, we will meet in heaven.

Your true friend,
Kin-na[3]

Upon his return to Africa, Kinna, one of the Amistad *rebels, wrote this letter to abolitionist Lewis Tappan.*

the people of your great kindness. . . . We will take the Bible with us. It has been a precious book, in prison, and we love to read it now we are free." They also sent a Bible to Adams as a gift for all he had done to help them.[4]

Once the *Gentleman* reached Africa, Cinqué headed for Mende country to find his family. But they had disappeared. He looked for them for many years.

Although a few of the other Africans stayed at the Sierra Leone mission, most found new lives on their own. One of the little girls, Margru, returned to the United States and attended Oberlin College in Ohio—the first to offer coeducational classes and to admit African Americans. Later, she went back to Africa to teach at the mission. Cinqué died there in 1879. In the meantime, the mission had been moved to Sherbro Island, off the coast of Sierra Leone, where it was maintained by the American Missionary Association, which not only established international missions but led the struggle to eliminate the slave trade.

The *Amistad* and the Slave Trade

Following the decision in the *Amistad* case, the Atlantic slave trade continued. However, the British were making a better effort to stop it. An average of twenty British ships patrolled the waters off west Africa, and a large part of the coastline had been shut down to the slave trade. Indeed, British naval authorities estimated that, between 1839 and 1850, they had captured seven hundred slaving vessels and reduced the number of slaves leaving for America by almost two thirds.[5] However, the United States government still did not allow American ships to be stopped by Great Britain in its search for illegal slave traders. Consequently, Spanish or Portuguese slavers would hoist an American flag to prevent British officials from searching their ships or seizing their cargo.

Because American slave ships could not be captured by Great Britain, the United States government eventually added its own warships to the African patrol. Their purpose was to end the external slave trade to America, which had been declared illegal in 1808. However, slavers continued to bring in their cargo illegally because the slave trade was still very profitable. There were so few American warships patrolling the African coast that they caught only a handful of American slavers. In addition, some United States officials, who were from the South, were reluctant to prosecute other Southerners after they were caught.

Meanwhile, the slave ships kept transporting their cargo to the Americas, which were a ready market for slaves. Agricultural expansion in Cuba, Brazil, and the American South increased the demand for slaves. Ships were outfitted in ports such as New York, New Orleans, and Charleston for the slave trade. Finally, the British sent several warships to Brazil in the late 1840s, and they succeeded in capturing and burning some of the slave ships. This was the beginning of the end for the Brazilian slave trade.

Nevertheless, slaves continued to reach the United States, where they were sold at auctions in the South to work on the plantations. The *Amistad* incident had awakened many people to the evils of the slave trade. But it would take the efforts of the British Navy as well as the American Civil War to finally bring the slave trade to an end.

The *Amistad* and Slavery

The Supreme Court's decision in the *Amistad* case had very little impact on the institution of slavery. The Court ruled that the captives were not slaves, and therefore, they should not be returned to Cuba. However, the justices did nothing to overturn the principle that slaves in America were considered property. Indeed, the Court ordered that Antonio—the slave who had belonged to the captain of the *Amistad*—should be returned to Cuba. He was later rescued by abolitionists and eventually went to live in Canada. Meanwhile, abolitionists continued their efforts to overturn the institution of slavery.

At first considered a fringe group of extremists, the abolitionists eventually gathered greater support in the North and helped form the Free-Soil party, which nominated Martin Van Buren as its candidate for president in 1848. Van Buren had been forgiven for his role in the *Amistad* incident, and his fame as an ex-president seemed to make him a strong candidate.

Although he became very unpopular among abolitionists because of his role in the Amistad *case, Martin Van Buren remained politically influential and even ran again for president.*

Free-Soilers wanted to stop the spread of slavery into new territories, fearing the political power of the South if the number of slave states increased. The United States had conquered a large western territory during the Mexican War (1846–1848) and this area became a battleground between proslavery and antislavery forces, especially when California petitioned for admission to the Union as a free state in 1850. Southerners wanted to extend slavery into these territories, while Northern political leaders were opposed. The two sides did not want to upset the balance of power in Congress, which was fairly evenly divided between proslavery and antislavery forces. Eventually, Congress agreed on a compromise. The Compromise of 1850 allowed California to enter the Union as a free state. At the same time, the settlers in the territories of New Mexico and Utah would vote on whether to allow slavery. This concept was called popular sovereignty.

For a time, a larger conflict between the North and the South over the issue of slavery seemed to have been avoided. But when the 1854 Kansas-Nebraska Act was passed, hostilities began again. The act set up the territories of Kansas and Nebraska, allowing settlers in each to vote on whether or not to allow slavery. Settlers there began battling violently over the issue. One of the antislavery men who participated in this conflict, John Brown, later led a raid on the United States arsenal at Harpers Ferry, Virginia, hoping to steal military weapons, arm the slaves, and unleash a massive slave revolt. Although he was later hanged, Brown became a martyr in the North. However, his raid made Southerners more determined than ever to hold on to their system of slavery.

In 1860, Abraham Lincoln was elected president and pledged to oppose the expansion of slavery westward. Southern states began to secede, or leave the Union. A bloody civil war would finally decide the future of slavery and the Union of the states.

In 1865, after the North won the Civil War that had raged since 1861, Congress began to pass a series of laws that outlawed slavery in the United States and gave African Americans the same rights as other citizens. Despite these gains, discrimination continued. In the Southern states, "Jim Crow," or segregation, laws were passed that prevented African Americans from attending the same schools as whites, or eating in the same restaurants. African Americans were also prevented from voting in elections. This discrimination would not begin to be eliminated until the civil rights movement that took place in the middle of the twentieth century.

Although great progress had finally been made, the Atlantic slave trade left behind a legacy of racism and cruelty. Even today, nearly two hundred years after the *Amistad* case, the slave trade continues to show its effects, both in the United States and in Africa.

Timeline

1200s—Moorish traders sell black slaves in Europe.

1400s—Portuguese explorers sail along African coast and trade in slaves.

1510—Slaves begin arriving in Spanish America.

1619—First slaves arrive in Virginia.

1739—Stono Rebellion, led by a slave named Cato, is put down.

1740–1750—British merchants carry more than two hundred thousand slaves to the Americas.

1787—United States Constitutional Convention permits external slave trade until 1808.

1791—Toussaint L'Ouverture leads a slave revolt in Haiti.

1793—Eli Whitney invents the cotton gin.

1800—Slave revolt led by Gabriel Prosser is put down.

1821—American Colonization Society founds Liberia for freed slaves; Denmark Vesey leads an unsuccessful slave revolt in South Carolina.

1831—William Lloyd Garrison begins publishing *The Liberator*; Nat Turner is hanged after leading a failed slave revolt.

1833—Great Britain abolishes slavery in its colonies in the West Indies.

1836—Martin Van Buren is elected president.

1839—Joseph Cinqué is captured in Sierra Leone and transported to Cuba as a slave; Cinqué leads a slave revolt aboard the *Amistad*; The *Amistad* is captured off Long Island by U.S.S. *Washington*; Cinqué and the other captives are put in jail in New London, Connecticut; Circuit court hears *Amistad* case.

1840—United States district court rules that Cinqué and the other Africans are free and cannot be held as slaves; Government appeals to the United States Supreme Court.

1841—Supreme Court hears the *Amistad* case; Court rules that Africans must be set free; Cinqué and other Africans return to Africa.

1846–1848—Mexican War is fought; America gains western territories.

1850—Compromise of 1850 retains balance between proslavery and antislavery states.

1854—Proslavery and antislavery forces begin battling in the territories of Kansas and Nebraska.

1859—John Brown leads a failed raid on the arsenal at Harpers Ferry, Virginia; Brown is hanged.

1860—Abraham Lincoln is elected president; South Carolina secedes from the Union.

1861–1865—American Civil War is fought, ending in a Northern victory.

1865—Slaves are freed by the Thirteenth Amendment to the Constitution.

1879—Joseph Cinqué dies in Africa.

Chapter Notes

Chapter 1. Rebellion!

1. Daniel Mannix, *Black Cargoes: A History of the Atlantic Slave Trade, 1518–1865* (New York: Viking, 1962), p. 231.

2. Thomas Howard, ed., *Black Voyage: Eyewitness Accounts of the Atlantic Slave Trade* (Boston: Little, Brown and Company, 1971), p. 3.

3. Olaudah Equiano, *The Life of Olaudah Equiano, or Gustavus Vassa the African* (Essex, England: Longman, 1988), p. 25.

4. Howard Jones, *Mutiny on the "Amistad": The Saga of a Slave Revolt and Its Impact on American Abolition, Law, and Diplomacy* (New York: Oxford, 1987), p. 23.

5. Doug Linder, "Newspaper Accounts of the Amistad Case," *Amistad Trial Page*, n.d., <http://www.law.umk.edu/faculty/projects/ftrials/amistad/AMI_NEWS.HTM> (July 7, 2000).

Chapter 2. The Middle Passage

1. Aristotle, *The Works of Aristotle* (Chicago: Encyclopedia Britannica, Inc., 1952), vol. 2, p. 447.

2. Hugh Thomas, *The Slave Trade: The Story of the Atlantic Slave Trade, 1440–1870* (New York: Simon & Schuster, 1997), p. 41.

3. Olaudah Equiano, *The Life of Olaudah Equiano, or Gustavus Vassa the African* (Essex, England: Longman, 1988), pp. 9–10.

4. Thomas, p. 69.

5. Ibid., p. 182.

6. Ibid., p. 185.

7. Ibid., pp. 264, 370.

8. Paul Halsall, "Venture Smith relates the story of his kidnapping at the age of six (1798)," *Internet Modern History Sourcebook*, June–August 1998, <http://vi.uh.edu/pages/mintz/4.htm> (July 7, 2000).

9. Thomas Howard, ed., *Black Voyage: Eyewitness Accounts of the Atlantic Slave Trade* (Boston: Little, Brown and Company, 1971), p. 120.

10. Paul Halsall, "A European slave trader, John Barbot, describes the African slave trade (1682)," *Internet African History Sourcebook*, June–August 1998, <http://vi.uh.edu/pages/mintz/1.htm> (July 7, 2000).

11. Howard, pp. 122–123.

12. Ibid., p. 80.

13. Ibid., p. 131.

14. Madeleine Burnside, *Spirits of the Passage: The Transatlantic Slave Trade in the Seventeenth Century* (New York: Simon and Schuster, 1997), p. 134.

15. Paul Halsall, "A European slave trader, James Bardot, Jr., describes a shipboard slave revolt by enslaved Africans (1700)," *Internet African History Sourcebook*, June–August 1998, <http://vi.uh.edu/pages/mintz/5.htm> (July 7, 2000).

16. Burnside, p. 125.

17. Thomas, p. 639.

18. John W. Blassingame, ed., *Slave Testimony: Two Centuries of Letters, Speeches, Interviews, and Autobiographies* (Baton Rouge: Louisiana State University Press, 1977), pp. 242–243.

Chapter 3. The *Amistad* and American Slavery

1. Hugh Thomas, *The Slave Trade: The Story of the Atlantic Slave Trade, 1440–1870* (New York: Simon & Schuster, 1997), p. 527.

2. Daniel Mannix, *Black Cargoes: A History of the Atlantic Slave Trade, 1518–1865* (New York: Viking, 1962), p. 194.

3. Warren S. Howard, *American Slavers and the Federal Law, 1837–1862* (Berkeley: University of California Press, 1963), pp. 17–18.

4. Ibid., p. 111.

5. Edward Ball, *Slaves in the Family* (New York: Ballantine Books, 1999), p. 190.

6. Ibid., p. 89.

7. Peter Kolchin, *American Slavery, 1619–1877* (New York: Hill and Wang, 1993), p. 11.

8. Mannix, p. 160.

9. Kolchin, p. 57.

10. John W. Blassingame, ed., *Slave Testimony: Two Centuries of Letters, Speeches, Interviews, and Autobiographies* (Baton Rouge: Louisiana State University Press, 1977), pp. 219–220.

11. Mannix, p. 187.
12. Ball, p. 264.
13. Kolchin, p. 93.

Chapter 4. Igniting the Firestorm

1. Doreen Carvajal, "Slavery's Truths (and Tales) Come Flocking Home," *The New York Times*, March 28, 1999.

2. Truman Nelson, ed., *Documents of Upheaval: Selections from William Lloyd Garrison's "The Liberator," 1831–1865* (New York: Hill and Wang, 1966), p. 28.

3. Helen Kromer, *Amistad: The Slave Uprising Aboard the Spanish Schooner* (Cleveland: The Pilgrim Press, 1997), pp. 39–40.

4. Howard Jones, *Mutiny on the Amistad* (New York: Oxford University Press, 1987), pp. 48–49.

5. *New York Morning Herald*, September 13, 1939 (from *"Amistad": A True Story of Freedom*, an exhibit at the Connecticut Historical Society, Hartford, Connecticut).

6. Alexis de Tocqueville, *Democracy in America* (New York: Knopf, 1994), p. 359.

7. Jones, p. 57.

Chapter 5. The Trials Begin

1. Howard Jones, *Mutiny on the Amistad* (New York: Oxford University Press, 1987), p. 66.

2. Dwight L. Dumond, ed., *Letters of James Gillespie Birney, 1831–1857* (New York: Appleton Century, 1938), vol. 1, p. 499.

3. *New London Gazette and Advertiser*, September 4, 1839 (from *"Amistad": A True Story of Freedom*, an exhibit at the Connecticut Historical Society, Hartford, Connecticut).

4. *The Southern Patriot*, Charleston, South Carolina, September 10, 1839 (from *"Amistad: A True Story of Freedom"*).

5. John Barber, *A History of the Amistad Captives* (New York: Arno Press, 1969), p. 16.

6. Jones, p. 76.

7. Clifton Johnson, *The Amistad Case and Its Consequences in U.S. History* (New Orleans: The Amistad Research Center, 1999), p. 5.

8. Jones, pp. 111–112.

9. Barber, pp. 20–21.

10. Johnson, p. 9.

Chapter 6. The *Amistad* and the Supreme Court

1. John W. Blassingame, ed., *Slave Testimony: Two Centuries of Letters, Speeches, Interviews, and Autobiographies* (Baton Rouge: Louisiana State University, 1977), p. 33.
2. Ibid.
3. Paul C. Nagel, *John Quincy Adams: A Public Life, a Private Life* (New York: Knopf, 1997), p. 356.
4. Allan Nevins, ed., *The Diary of John Quincy Adams, 1794–1845* (New York: Scribner's, 1951), p. 516.
5. Ibid., p. 519.
6. John Quincy Adams, *Argument in the Case of United States vs. Cinque* (New York: Arno Press, 1969), p. 6.
7. Adams, p. 12.
8. Ibid., p. 38.
9. *Argument of John Quincy Adams*, n.d., <http://www.multied.com/amistad/amistad.html> (July 7, 2000).
10. *The Philanthropist*, Cincinnati, Ohio, March 3, 1841.
11. Blassingame, pp. 42–43.

Chapter 7. The *Amistad* in History

1. *The Philanthropist*, Cincinnati, Ohio, December 29, 1841.
2. John W. Blassingame, ed., *Slave Testimony: Two Centuries of Letters, Speeches, Interviews, and Autobiographies* (Baton Rouge: Louisiana State University Press, 1977), p. 42.
3. Doug Linder, "Letter from Kin-na to Tappan," *Amistad Trial Page*, n.d., <http://www.law.umk.edu/faculty/projects/ftrials/amistad/AMI_LTR.HTM> (July 7, 2000).
4. Blassingame, p. 43.
5. Daniel Mannix, *Black Cargoes: A History of the Atlantic Slave Trade, 1518–1865* (New York: Viking Press, 1962), p. 264.

Further Reading and Internet Addresses

Books

Altman, Linda Jacobs. *Slavery and Abolition in American History*. Berkeley Heights, N.J.: Enslow Publishers, Inc., 1999.

Cable, Mary. *Black Odyssey: The Case of the Slave Ship Amistad*. New York: Penquin Books, 1971.

Paulson, Timothy J. *Days of Sorrow, Years of Glory 1813–1850: From the Nat Turner Revolt to the Fugitive Slave Law.* New York: Chelsea House, 1994.

Stein, R. Conrad. *John Brown's Raid on Harpers Ferry in American History.* Springfield, N.J.: Enslow Publishers, Inc., 1999.

Walker, Jane C. *John Quincy Adams*. Berkeley Heights, N.J.: Enslow Publishers, Inc., 2000.

Zeinert, Karen. *The Amistad Slave Revolt & American Abolition.* North Haven, Conn.: Shoe String Press, Inc., 1997.

Internet Addresses

Amistad Trial Page. n.d. <http://www.law.umkc.edu/faculty/projects/ftrials/amistad/AMISTD.htm> (September 21, 2000.).

"Argument of John Quincy Adams." *HistoryCentral.com*. n.d. <http://www.multied.com/amistad/amistad.html> (July 7, 2000).

Halsall, Paul. *Internet Modern History Sourcebook*. June–August 1998. <http://www.fordham.edu/halsall/mod/modsbook.html> (September 21, 2000).

Index